How To Buy a Car

Without Losing Your Shirt

by Jay Hamilton

INCLUDES BONUS CONTENT

from our new book

COMPOSITION:

Book One of John Waaser's Photography Course

COVER ART:

Concept of salesman as Vulture with Customer's
Shirt Over His Left Shoulder by

the Author

Execution by

Michael Garvin, Gainesville, FL

TABLE OF CONTENTS

ABOUT THE AUTHOR

Jay Hamilton has two decades of experience as a freelance motorsports journalist, and has been an elected officer of a sports car club, as well as Publicity Director, Newsletter Editor, and other officer positions in two different motorcycle clubs. His work has been published in National Magazines such as "Cycle Guide" and "Modern Cycle." He has also had photos published in "Cycle" Magazine. In addition, he has worked as parts, service, and warranty claims manager in two small sports car shops, and been a service writer in a much larger dealership, as well as a salesman, in several dealerships in more than one state. He has full knowledge of the working principles behind these dealerships. The stress involved in selling cars was a bit much for him, however. With this background, he felt he should write a book to explain to customers, the steps involved in selling a new car, and how to get out of there with a pretty good deal, including after-sales service—generally not covered in this type of book by other authors. This book also goes into financing the car and other areas which are necessarily a part of purchasing a new or used car.

Crossroads Publishing is the coming together of three different names who all were well-known motorsports journalists at the same time and at the same events. We will be doing cookbooks, photography courses, how-to books of all types (including some gardening and off-grid stuff), and some fiction as well. This is our first effort at publishing, but certainly not our last.

Thank you for purchasing this book! And congratulations on making this the first step in learning how to buy a car without losing your shirt. If you feel anything in this book has been able to save you more than the cost of the book, please leave a favorable review on the website where you purchased the book. This is a long book, about double the length of other books I've seen on this subject, and I cover some areas they don't cover, and I go deeper into those areas which they do cover. Most of the others who write about this subject, have been higher-ups in the dealership industry, and were responsible for the way their dealership was run, and it may still be in their interest to see you pay more than you should for your next vehicle. I remember the first article I saw on this subject, it was decades ago in a very popular magazine, and it suggested you should ask for a nominal discount only, on dealer-installed accessories. Nothing in that article would have gotten you to make an offer that would have given the dealer less than his average profit. In other words, he was helping the dealers make money at your expense. Some of the other books on this subject are in the same mode as that article. Most of the information in this book applies equally well to motorcycle dealers, boat dealers, recreational vehicle dealers, and even to mobile home dealers, and so on.

After you finish reading this book, go out and practice buying a car before you buy one for real

CHAPTER 1:

GENERAL INFORMATION

When you walk into a car dealership to look at a new car, who do you think has the advantage? Does the customer have the advantage, since he has the money? Not on your life! Even if you buy a new car every two or three years, the salesman who is about to greet you talks to three or four customers EVERY DAY! He has this down to a science and you don't. This booklet cannot make you a wonder buyer. The thing you must do is to be firm, and remember everything in this booklet, and that will be difficult. It would not hurt a bit to practice, with someone else playing the role of the salesman. (Role-playing is one of the first things a new car salesman does, before they turn him loose on the sales floor.) It might not even hurt a bit to "buy" a few cars from other dealers before you go to the dealer you want to buy from. Repeat players have all of the advantages, and you want to turn yourself into a repeat player before you play for real.

Choosing a dealer may be even more important than choosing the car, and the chances are you could live with something other than your dream model car if the dealership were more attentive. You should ask all of your friends who have bought cars lately what they think of the dealers they bought from.

You should find out if there is a high turnover of personnel at the dealership. That is a common problem in the automotive industry. If the salesman leaves the dealership a month or two after you buy a new car, you have lost a lot of leverage. The salesman will ask you to send him any friends who are about to buy a car— and he means to send them to him personally, not just to the dealership. This is because he is paid a commission on every car he sells. That commission is not like the commission a salesman in a retail store might get, of about 5% of the purchase price. The car salesman gets a commission of 25 – 30 per cent of the Gross Profit on the deal. The more money he makes for the dealership, the more he puts in his pocket—and he gets a considerable chunk of the difference. If you send him a few customers, he earns a lot of money by keeping you happy. Don't be shy about asking him for a referral fee, known in the trade as a "bird dog" fee. These days that fee is likely to be $100 per closed deal. It certainly should be no less than $50. It is best if you take your friend in there and personally introduce him, or at least call the salesman BEFORE the friend gets there, so there is no doubt that the reason this customer saw that salesman is because you sent him in. For your information, the bird dog fee is generally paid by the dealer and does not come out of the sales rep's commission. This kind of potential relationship is enough to keep the salesman who sold you the car, interested in any problems you have with the car after you get it home. If he leaves the dealership, you have a lot less leverage in case of problems.

For this reason, I do not recommend buying a car over the phone, or over the internet. I have seen books which advise you to talk only to the "internet salesperson." Poppycock! In dealerships where I have worked, every salesperson was entitled to sell over the internet, and from internet offerings I have seen, that appears to be a common thread. But if there were an internet-only salesperson, they would most likely not be on commission, they would be a low-salaried employee, with little knowledge about cars and/or the workings of the dealership. They would be simply an order-taker, not capable of helping you choose a model that is right for you or anything else. Also, like dealerships which advertise that every vehicle is pre-priced, and their sales people are not on commission, the price includes an average markup, which gives the dealer the kind of profit he expects to make on every deal, and you want to hold him to less profit than that. If you read this book through, and understand the process, and get some practice before you negotiate for real, you should have no problem in working the dealer down to a much lower profit than those single-priced dealerships, or internet salespeople, will be permitted to offer you.

It goes without saying, that because of the way the salesman gets paid, you should always talk to the same salesman every time you return to the dealer. It has become apparent to me that many customers do not realize this. But that salesman will get to know you, and—as we already noted—he will be your strongest ally in the dealership, should a problem develop. Suppose you talk to one salesman a couple of times, and then buy from someone else: the first salesman has essentially wasted every minute he spent with you. If you come back with a problem, he will NOT want to talk to you, PERIOD! If, on the other hand, you always talked to the same salesman you bought from, and he is not there when you come in with a problem, someone else may be willing to help with your problem, because they would want someone to help THEIR customer under similar circumstances. Solving a problem after the sale is not a waste of time. It is a duty they owe to the dealership. But talking to someone who later buys from someone else IS a waste of time, and a salesman who has wasted time with you before the purchase, will not want to know you after the purchase. Other salesmen may also be aware of your fickleness.

If, on the other hand, you don't like the salesman with whom you are talking, you should ask to see the sales manager, and explain this to him as soon as you become aware of your feelings. Every salesperson has their own style, and most dealerships will keep people from a variety of backgrounds there. It is far from unheard of that a particular customer will not like one particular salesperson from time to time. But generally, there will be some hard feelings somewhere, if one salesperson wastes a significant amount of time with a customer who then buys from another salesperson at the same dealership. The customer may wind up being one of the ones hurt by those hard feelings, so please, Please, PLEASE always talk to the same salesperson whenever you go into a particular dealership. If you don't see him, ASK for that person by name. You both will generally be better off that way. Normally, if another salesperson writes a deal after you have asked for your salesperson, the two will split the commission. It would be best if you CALL your salesperson, and ensure that (s)he will be there when you plan to arrive. Unless the shop is unusually busy, (s)he will try to avoid talking to anyone else within an hour or so of any appointment. Of course, if (s)he has left the dealership, you might want to know why, and where (s)he has gone to (something the dealership might be reluctant to tell you, since it could cost them business.)

Once, I had to leave to go to a locksmith to pick up a key, when we could not find the key for something I was selling. When I arrived back, I saw a regular, steady customer of mine in the showroom. I waved to him; he lit up in a huge grin, and waved back. As I walked out of the closing room again for a second, I told him that I would be right with him. I then noticed on the computer that another salesman was working with him. This other salesman was (in my well-considered opinion) a pathological liar. I immediately walked up to my customer, and asked him whether he had asked for me when he first came in. He replied that he had wanted to talk to me, that he had asked for me, and that he had been told simply that I was not there. The other salesman absolutely insisted that that the customer did not ask for any salesman when he first walked up to the customer. I have waited on that customer practically every time he came in to the shop, even for parts. I had the kind of relationship where I am certain that the customer would not walk into the shop without my name on his lips. He was looking at a particular model, which he had discussed with me earlier. We had the 1993 model, which had come in since he had last talked to me, in the back under wraps until we sold the 1992 unit that we had in stock. I know that this customer wanted the '92 over the '91 when he bought his trade. I certainly would have told him that we had the '93 in stock. Instead, the other salesman made him a deal on the '92, without telling him that the '93 was in. Ultimately the deal fell through, probably because the customer sensed that the other sales rep was lying about whether the customer had asked for me, since the other salesman wanted to keep the deal for himself, rather than splitting it with me. The commission on the deal was approximately $160, so the salesman was lying for about $80. The boss will not call the customer to verify the truth. I probably will ultimately quit, and if I do, this incident will have a lot to do with it. (Actually, I did quit, and started my own computer store, a short while later, after the same salesman pulled similar stunts on both myself and the third salesman in the shop. Once he even told a customer that the third salesman was gone, "but he'll be back in a (sic) hour…" The other salesman had gone home to watch a major race on television, and had said he might be back before closing, but he was having friends over, and there were sure to be martinis involved, and nobody expected to see him return. When the customer came back, this guy started a deal in the computer, telling the customer that it was just roughed in, and that his regular salesman would finalize things like the trade allowance. This customer, a retired professor, was buying four or five vehicles a year from one particular salesman in this dealership. Store rule was that the salesperson who started the deal in the computer owned the sale, and that if it was ultimately closed by another salesperson, the commission would be split. I couldn't wait to get out of there.) If you find yourself in a similar situation, and you perceive that one salesman has lied to you or about you, do everyone a favor, and speak to the owner of the business, and tell him WHY you will not do business there, and why you will not recommend that your friends do business there. Of course, if you still like your regular salesperson, you can calm down later and continue to do business with your regular salesperson….

The "Service Advisor" who greets you when you come in for service is also paid a commission on his sales, and it is therefore in his interest to sell you service that may not be necessary. If he knows that in the event he treats you properly, you will always come back to him, that represents repeat business which may in the end be more lucrative than stabbing you in the back. Again, if there is a high turnover of service writers, you will lose that leverage.

Advertising is viewed by car dealers as simply a way to get customers to the lot. The sales process does not begin until you get to see a salesperson. Dealers will flat lie in their advertising, and the salesman is taught to lie to you if you telephone in from an ad. They will say that a car, which is already sold, is still available, for instance, and if you put down the phone and race to the lot, they will say that another salesman just sold it after you called about it. Many dealers now advertise a price that is $2000 below the actual price, but there is fine print, which says "with $2000 cash down or trade equity." The price is so much lower than other dealers are advertising the same car for, that you are bound to notice, and to visit this dealership—probably first on your list. That is the whole purpose of advertising. Remember that this is a numbers game. For every four people he gets on the lot, the dealer will sell about one car right away. He can expect to sell at least one of the others later, if his salespeople do their follow-up correctly. His primary concern with advertising is to get you on the lot. He doesn't care if his advertising is honest. The courts will allow a little "puffing" because you are expected to notice the puffing. Caveat Emptor (Buyer Beware) is still the basis for the legal system in this country, even in those states with strong consumer protection laws. Most of those laws don't really have the teeth the legislators thought they would have when they passed the laws, and they certainly don't have the teeth the consumers thought they would have when the news outlets ran stories on these laws. DO NOT TRUST A DEALER'S ADVERTISING!

The basis of the legal system in this country, when it comes to commerce, is something called the Uniform Commercial Code, or at least that is supposed to be the basis. Part of that code is the concept that there is an implied warranty of merchantability, and of fitness for the intended purpose. I recently discovered that there are ten or a dozen states in this country where all the dealer must do is to include the words "As Is" on the bill of sale, and in those states

(Florida is one of them), those four letters and one space, wipe out the implied warranties guaranteed by the Uniform Commercial Code. This is a rip-off, and occurs in states where the automobile dealership lobby owns the state legislature, and this is true even in states which try to tell you that they have strong consumer protection laws (like Florida.) I would hazard a guess that most of these states are traditional Republican strongholds. Do a search using your favorite search engine, for "implied warranties in (your state)." There should be some consumer-oriented law firms in the state with websites dealing with this subject, and they should come right up when you enter that search string. This applies predominately to used car sales, since new cars are warrantied nationwide by the manufacturer.

We said that the dealership has the art of selling you a car down to a science. They keep records so detailed that they can tell which salesperson has the best close ratio for first visit customers, and which salesperson works the hardest to get unsold customers back into the dealership, and so on. There are also several STEPS in dealing with each customer that are practiced religiously by all car dealers. These steps may vary slightly because the dealer subscribes to a sales organization that tells him how to best turn a prospect into a sold unit, and those organizations vary slightly in what they tell the dealers to do.

Those sales organizations also break down their dealers into groups of ten to twenty dealerships, usually based on demographics of the dealer's locale. These might be called a "Twenty Club," or whatever. One of the dealers I worked for belonged to a sales group that I called "The Lemmings." Oddly enough, one of the other dealers in his 20 club was a guy I had known personally, a couple of decades earlier. Each month, usually on, say, the third Thursday of each month, but generally the same day of the week, and about the same time of the month, all twenty of them will descend on one of their dealerships, and break down what the dealer is doing right, or perhaps wrong. If this dealer has found something that works well, he will show it off, and the others may copy him. If someone spots something he's doing wrong, they will bring it to his attention, and suggest ways to improve the situation. Often, the companies who own these businesses that show dealers how to run their dealerships, are guys who have lost one or more of their own dealerships!

Often, they hire a psychiatrist to script their sales routine. In some cases, sales people will be ordered to follow the script word for word, while in other cases, they may have more freedom to divert, as long as they cover the bases. But there will be key words that the psychiatrist has assured them will break down resistance. It would be interesting to record an audio transcript of the entire sales pitch, to see if other dealers will be using the same script. I will try to get a blog up shortly after this book is published so that people from all over the country can upload such recordings for comparison, or upload notes with specific quotes that seemed a bit out of line, so that other buyers can listen for early clues that their dealers are about to unleash something dishonest on them.

CHAPTER 2:

THE FIVE BASIC STEPS IN SELLING A CAR

1:   Greet the customer

Never say anything to which the customer can logically respond in the negative. For instance, if the salesman were to say "Can I help you?" the customer might respond with a simple "No," or "Just looking," or perhaps even a grammar correction like "You probably can, but you may not!" The salesman is taught to greet you in a way that requires a response, to start a conversation rolling, like "Good morning. Welcome to our dealership." It would be rude of you not to respond to that. (And, of course, there are indeed some customers who are rude enough to totally ignore a salesman attempting to start a conversation in that manner….) If he is really good, he will ask you something, or make a statement, that requires a response from you, like "You're lucky to find one of those models on our lot. We can't keep them in stock. Which color would you prefer?"

Incidentally, that last approach illustrates another fact you will discover in visiting car dealerships. The salesman is taught to offer you a choice, but not an unlimited choice. "Would you prefer the blue one or the beige one?" "Would you like delivery on Wednesday afternoon, or would Thursday morning be better for you?" If one of those is really better for you, you will tell him so, and you have made a small commitment every time you do so. If neither choice is acceptable, but you respond with an alternative that is acceptable to you, you have made an even larger commitment.

At this point, the salesman will begin to ask you enough questions to determine which car you want, and perhaps to rule out certain ones. He will then decide on just one or two cars on the lot to show you. If he gives you too large a choice, you will have difficulty making up your mind later. If he does his job properly, he will choose a car you can live with. If he tries to show you the wrong car, don't hesitate to tell him so.

At some point, you will be taken on a tour of the dealership, and introduced to some key people in the parts and service departments, to make you think of these people as people you know, or even as your friends. This may be done at the greeting stage, but more likely after the test drive, when they are walking you into the closing room to negotiate the deal.

You will be asked many questions, to which the expected response will be "yes." This is to get you into the habit of saying "yes" to the salesperson. This could happen during the greeting, or the walk-around, or the test drive, or even as negotiations are just getting underway.

2: Walk around the car, pointing out features.

Usually, the sales rep will back the car out of the line before doing this step. That makes it easier to walk around the car, and to open the doors and such. But there is another reason for this stunt: it makes this car special. It makes it stand out from the other cars in the area. It is an effort to make you think of this car as YOURS!

For every feature, the salesman will also point out the benefit of that feature. "This car has our new electronically fuel-injected engine, which will start easier and get better fuel economy." Heck, that's TWO benefits. Notice he neglected to tell you that it also costs a lot more to service, and might require towing if the injection's computer system quits, whereas a car might run poorly, but still run, if a carburetor gets dirty. He will do this sort of thing all the way around the car, and tell you why this car is superior not only to his product of a few years ago, but also to his competitor's product of today. You should listen to him, of course, and ask questions if you have any, but do not be too impressed. Impressing you is what this step is all about.

3: Get the customer to DRIVE the car.

A test drive is the most important step of the selling effort. You cannot sell a car and make a lot of money on it unless the customer WANTS the car. The test drive instills desire in the customer. When the customer drives the car, he will get all of the sensations of a new car. He will notice the odor (some of which may have come in a spray can); he will notice how tight and new everything feels, and, by comparison, how ancient and decrepit his old clunker is. After the test drive, the customer will WANT the new car. But the test drive is also well orchestrated. The salesman will drive off the lot, and to a predetermined point, at which he will switch drivers. Initially, he may not even offer to let you drive the car, and may not even tell you that you are going for a test drive. He may just tell you to get in on the passenger side, and then he may hop into the driver's side and start driving. As he drives, he will point out the nice quiet ride, and so on. When his spiel is finished, he will then pull over and get out, then walk over to the passenger side, open the door, and tell you to hop over into the driver's seat and drive it back to the lot. The test drive induces DESIRE in the customer. Don't you fall for it. No matter how much you want the car after the test drive, remember that the price is still very negotiable.

You might also discover that you hate the car, and that you should be looking at something else! Many customers are reluctant to drive a new car. I have never been able to understand this, since I would not make such a significant purchase without trying it out first. But the salesman's goal is to point out the good features. Your job is to look for the things that you do NOT like about the car. Can you really live with this car for the next five years? Try to find points that would help you negotiate the price downward. And if you really think you should be looking at something else, you should explain that to the salesperson immediately.

4: Negotiate and close.

The salesperson will bring you into a private office to negotiate and close the deal. This is where you are in the most danger, and are the most vulnerable. If the salesperson has done the job well, you are now ready to pay any price for the car. Don't believe ANYTHING the salesperson or the sales manager tells you that they cannot verify from an unimpeachable source. For instance, we offered rustproofing "at our cost—when it was about double our cost, even after adding in the service department's profit. (The materials and labor—by the lowest guy on the totem pole in the service department—cost the dealership about $30. The service department sold it to the sales department for about $80, and we retailed it in about the $300 to $350 area, then willingly discounted it to about $180, and if the customer still balked at that price, offered it to the customer at "our cost" of about $130.) A friend of an ex-boss of mine came in one day, just to look around, and when he discovered that I was working there, he sent his sister to see me about an Olds Cutlass Supreme. She kept chewing us down, and chewing us down. I don't even know how she did it, but the price just kept getting lower and lower, and what had looked like a decent deal was fast evaporating away. Finally, with only $200-$300 in commissionable gross profit left, the sales manager said to me, "Whatever I say to her, you just agree with it!" I promised I would, and we went back to my closing booth to talk to her about her latest offer. The manager came back with a counter offer, and turned to me. "Now, you understand that this is such a rock bottom deal that we can't pay you any commission on it. You agree that because she is a friend of yours, you are willing to forego the commission just to sell her a car at an unbeatable price, right?" And he turned to her to make sure she understood that this was as low as we could go, and the only way we could go that low was because I was willing to lose my commission to put the deal together. Later I told her that I needed one more deal for the month to make my quota, or something like that. When she came in to pick up the car, she brought me a Cross pen as a gift, to make up for the lost commission. I made a commission on the deal— smaller than I was used to, but it was at least $50, which was double the minimum that they were paying back then. But she firmly believed that I had lost my commission because that's what the manager had said. Well, he lied. But that's par for the course in an automobile dealership, believe me.

When the salesperson goes to "touch desk" with the customer's first offer, he should come back with a complete set of figures, including, at minimum, the price of the new car, trade-in value of any used car you might be trading, the payoff on the used car, if any, and the final difference that must be paid in cash or financed. Recently I worked for a very short while at a small-town dealer who belonged to a sales group that had had psychiatrists interview people who had just bought new cars. They had a whole slew of specific phrases we had to use with every customer. We were told to ask every customer right off the bat, during the greet phase, "What do you like about your current car?" and especially, 'What do you not like about your current car?" Then we could point out how the new car solves the things that he did not like about the present one, and how the new car would enhance the things that he did like about his present vehicle. This was probably most done during the test drive, but to some degree, in the walk-around as well. But the real kicker was that the manager would send us out of the office with only three numbers, all of which were monthly payment figures, and all of which were at least double what the customer might reasonably have been expecting to pay. The purpose of that was to break the customer's thought stream. When we peeled the customer off the ceiling, the only numbers we would discuss after that were monthly payment figures. This dealership financed every deal in house, through a larger than normal string of finance companies. And when he got the customer to agree on a monthly payment figure at which he would buy the car, the dealer wrote the deal in the way that offered the most profit to the dealership. In the three weeks I toughed it out there, I talked to at least two customers who wanted to trade a vehicle they had bought there. In both cases, they were so upside down on their balance due on the loan, they could not trade that vehicle until within about six months of the time it would have been paid for in full! If you ever find a salesperson who uses this approach, stand up, demand the keys to your trade back, and any deposit you may have sent in with the first offer, and get the heck out of there! These are smaller dealers, who can only expect to sell about sixty cars per month, and they want to make just as much profit as a dealer who sells 150 cars per month. There is simply no way that you are going to get a satisfactory deal out of such a dealer! In my humble opinion, the failure to disclose all pertinent figures, so that the customer can compare them with other dealers on a similar vehicle, is simply dishonest, and you do not want to do business with anyone who is that dishonest!

You may want to have a car built that is similar to the one that you drove, but with a few differences, to make it all yours, just the way you want it. The salesman would rather sell you a car that is on the lot, or at least to swap cars with another dealership that has one closer to what you want. This way he can deliver it quicker, and avoid what is called "buyer remorse." A customer who orders a car might have second thoughts about the monthly payments, or might even go shopping elsewhere to convince himself that he really got a good deal, and find another dealer ready to beat it. Besides, the salesman is counting on this commission, and he wants it now! It is nothing for a salesman to make $400 to $800 on an individual deal if he does his job well, and he could make over a thousand dollars, though his average might be closer to $200. There is usually a floor, or minimum commission, which was $25 to $50 back in the day, but could be in the $75 to $100 range now, depending on the dealership. Thus the salesman is paid for his time, even if the dealership makes no profit at all on the deal. Obviously, you want to keep the salesman at the low end of this range. I did sell an Olds Cutlass Sedan to a local attorney, only to have him buy a similar Pontiac that was in stock at the Pontiac dealership, so he could drive his new car earlier than the one he had special-ordered, even though the special-order car was built exactly to his personal specifications. I had thought it was a good deal, but I lost it due to buyer remorse.

Once you have settled on the right car, the exact car you are negotiating on, the dickering starts in earnest. There is an old saying that "The first one who states a figure, loses." The dealer is very skilled at obtaining an offer from the customer. The salesman will quote you the full retail price, and wait for a response. If you don't ask for a discount, he will start writing it up and ask you to set a delivery date. If you balk at full retail, (or full retail less his initial offer on your trade-in) he will then ask what you think the car is worth.

He might laugh off your first offer, and cut the full retail by a little bit to see if you say yes. Often the customer has no idea what discounts are available, and the customer will fold early in the negotiation process. The salesperson doesn't know whether you expect a $200 discount, or a $5000 discount. If he offers you the car for $1000 off, and all you expected was $200, you will get confused, and want to go elsewhere to see what deals you can be offered. On the other hand, if you expected a $2000 discount, and he only offers you $600 off, you might leave in a huff. He WANTS your offer first, to see where you stand on this. He also will ask you for a strong deposit, "since that is such a low offer it is unlikely to be accepted, but the strongest possible deposit will show the owners that you are serious, and give you more leverage." The offer is not legal without a tender, but you could offer him a $1 deposit to make the offer legal in most states. He'll ask for a minimum of $200 in most dealerships, because at that figure, if you don't go through with the deal, it will cost you a sum that most people don't want to lose. You can offer him a large deposit ($1000 or more) if you have made a truly low offer on a car you really want, but otherwise, try to give him a deposit of ten dollars. Then he will go to the office with your offer, your deposit, and the keys to your trade-in, if any. He will come back from the office with a denial. Even if you offered $200 below retail, he wants you to have to fight for that offer, so you think you got the best deal that you could have gotten. He will also leave your deposit and your keys in the office. This is so that if you are ready to leave, he can get a sales manager (a stronger negotiator than himself) to come out to return your deposit and keys, and they get a second chance to negotiate with you. I told you that this was well orchestrated. I once went in with an offer of $200 off the price on a self-contained van-based motor home, very proud of myself, expecting a fast signature from the manager, since we had been sitting on that thing forever. Instead he came out with me, and flat told the little old lady that we couldn't sell it that low, and we got just about full retail out of it!

Incidentally, the offer is not binding on the dealership unless it is signed by an officer of the dealership—at minimum the sales manager. The salesperson is not authorized to bind the dealership to any deal. If they give you a deal signed by the salesman only, you can't even use it to negotiate a better offer from another dealership. Such a stunt may be used if they think that you are going to shop the deal. Make sure it is signed by someone with the authority to bind the dealership.

When you finally agree on a price (or a trade difference) they will write it up and set up the delivery date. Then it is time to talk financing and such. The salesperson may do this in some shops, or they might turn you over to the "F & I Guy." If they have a separate Finance and Insurance Manager, you will be pressured very strongly to finance through the dealership, and possibly also to buy your insurance through the dealership. Insurance may mean just credit life insurance, or it may mean the entire automotive insurance package, depending on the state where the dealership is located, and the individual dealership. (In most states, they would have to employ a licensed insurance agent to sell you insurance, but they could also be paid a spiff by a local licensed agent who wants to write all of their insurance. When I was selling motorcycles, we had an agent who would come to the dealership to write full coverage insurance on every bike we sold, so that the financing would go through without a hitch.) The F&I Guy also gives the dealer a second chance to sell you items such as rustproofing, paint glaze, fabric treatment, radios, wheels and tires, and other high-profit items. Understand that that is his job, and that even after the price of the base vehicle is agreed upon, anything they add later is also highly negotiable, especially since these are the high-profit items. We sold Pinstriping, for instance, for five times what it cost us.

A phrase you are likely to hear often, especially during the negotiation stage, but possibly before that as well, is "What will it take for me to earn your business today?" The two most important words there are "earn," and 'today." He wants you to think that he has earned your business, and he wants it to happen today, and he wants you to think in those terms.

He also will frequently refer to the car as yours before you even sign, as in "What day would you like to take delivery of your new car?" That makes you think of the new car as yours before the negotiations are even complete. Be aware of this type of talk, and note that every time that he uses this language, he is just trying to make you think of the car as your own, and don't you fall for it!

5: Delivery.

Delivery is the most important part of the sale, and your salesperson will often schedule the delivery during his time off, so that he will not be bothered by anyone or anything else while he is delivering your car. In any event, NOTHING is supposed to take his attention away from you during the delivery. He will have personally checked to ensure that all of the work that was supposed to have been done to the car, and all of the paperwork, actually got done, before you arrive. He does not want you to have to wait for delivery, and he does not want something to go wrong. He wants this to be the proudest moment of your life, PERIOD! He wants you to take this beauty home and show it to all of your friends and send them to see HIM. If a problem crops up during delivery, and it is logically something that could have been checked previously, the salesperson was inexcusably lax.

One more thing: there is a practice now called "spot delivery." There is a lot of potential here to get a dealer in a LOT of trouble. When I was selling Toyotas in Massachusetts, NO car rolled until the check cleared, and the salesperson often had to run the check to the customer's bank to certify it. When I was selling Buicks in Florida, we delivered the cars the minute the customer signed the papers. You could hand me a personal check for $20,000 and drive away in a new car, in the evening, after the banks had all closed. You could even tell me that there were no funds in that account, and that you would transfer them tomorrow, and you could drive out in the car. Spot delivery is a means of eliminating "buyer remorse," and after-the-fact price shopping. But some bright guy could take delivery of two or three cars in one night, using phony ID, and then deliver them to a chop house, or for overseas sales, and get a five-figure cash payment for them. If he bought in several cities within the week, and then laid low for a while, he could earn a comfortable living doing just that. Spot delivery is a method of high-pressure sales that is stupid and irresponsible, and someday some dealer is going to get burned badly enough to make him reconsider doing spot deliveries. If the dealer pressures you to take delivery the first time you look at the car, I'd say he has a pretty insecure feeling about the deal. I'm not certain that from the customer's standpoint, there's anything really wrong with it, but there are some things that could go wrong. Does the dealer have the financing approved? REALLY approved? What happens if for some reason, you pick up the car on the spot, and the next day the finance company says no to the deal? That could easily happen, especially if any little thing has changed, like you added an entertainment package at the last minute, and the price went up accordingly. Just to make matters worse, let's say that he sold your trade the first thing the next morning, perhaps to another dealer. Now you have a car you must give back, but he doesn't have your trade-in. What now? Well, he gives you the cash value of your trade-in—at ACV (Actual Cash Value, not what he allowed for the car)—according to most of the dealer contracts I have seen. Or he can give you a "comparable" car—except that used cars are built one at a time, and there really is nothing "comparable" to be found.

Those five steps will be performed religiously by any dealership with any interest in making money on the sale. There will be records kept, and the salesman will have a follow-up schedule to call you every few days if you did not buy the car on the first visit to the dealership. You may also receive a call from the sales manager, supposedly attempting to check on the salesperson's performance. This gives the sales manager another attempt to get you back in, and he is usually the best salesman on the lot. He will be very persuasive. If your salesperson quits or gets fired, whoever is hired to replace him will call all of his old customers, or the list will be split among the regular sales people there. You will be called; you can be sure of that.

Bear in mind, however, that the customer has the money, so the customer can be in the driver's seat. All the customer has to do is assume control. I was, in fact, offered the job at the Toyota dealership because the sales rep was not able to control me. I did not ask about a job. I was photographing motorcycle races for a living, and having a wonderful time, and I was not looking for a job. They offered me the job because I maintained control while talking with one of their best salesmen. Don't be put off by the fact that the salesperson is more familiar with the steps of selling than you are. He is courting you and your money because you have something he wants even more than you want that new car. Keep that in mind at all times when dealing with the car dealership.

Incidentally, I had the best first-visit close ratio at the Toyota dealership, around 28%. That is, 28% of the customers who came into the dealership for the first time, and spoke to me, signed a deal at that time. The dealership average was about 22%. (The dealer's advertising slogan was [his name]—"Someone you can trust!" The owner used to walk up to me on the lot, and say [my name]— "Someone you can trust!" because it was obvious that the results I had were driven by the fact that people trusted me more than anyone else there.) A smaller percentage came back later and bought the car, while close to half bought elsewhere, and a few people never bought, possibly because they could not be financed. Well over half the people who venture into a dealership insist that they are just looking, and have no intention of buying a car on that day or any day. Salespeople have an expression: "Customers lie." That is clearly true, but you should remember that salespeople also lie—a lot!

I am told that in some areas of the country, some large dealers will have men in towers with binoculars, in radio contact with sales personnel—so you can come onto the lot, and look around, but if you start to leave, they nail you before you get off the lot. I really can't believe that such a thing happens, because it doesn't jibe with the numbers game. The dealer's best chance to slow the customer down is when the customer first walks onto the lot, not as the customer is leaving. Dealers who play this game will lose a lot of customers. If you see a dealer do this, you can assume that you will be high-pressured. The time to get off that lot is when the salesman first walks up to you as you are leaving.

One local dealer used to advertise a 3-day money-back guarantee. This means that he isn't transferring the title for three days or more. In some states he can get away with that. But when he takes the car back, he will probably try to sell it as new, and I feel that would be crooked as hell, even if you were, in fact, the first titled owner. Would you want to buy a car as new, only to discover that someone else had bought it, and returned it within three days, because they thought it was a lemon? Chrysler was once sued over executive use of "new" cars. How much different is this situation? I don't think I'd want to buy from a dealership that advertised this type of deal. For all it might be a safety valve, to allow you to return a lemon, it presents too much potential for abuse.

A new car should have only the factory miles on it, and any miles added as they loaded it and unloaded it during transportation from the factory. Somewhere around five miles is normal. If the dealer obtained the car in a dealer swap, there will be additional miles incurred there, perhaps 20 miles to a hundred or so, but rarely more than that. If the car was a demo unit for one of the firm's salespeople, it will have more miles than that, and the dealer will have received a demo allowance from the manufacturer, and the price should be dramatically reduced as a result. It is, then, a used car, even if it has never been titled and carries a full new car warranty. Any other mileage is abnormal, and should be fully explained. If this is a dealer who holds the title for any return period, I would be leery of buying any car that was initially delivered to this dealer (the original dealer will be listed on the manufacturer's invoice or on the window sticker) and that shows any abnormal mileage. If it was a swap car, you should be able to determine with some accuracy, the distance between the two dealerships, and determine if the mileage is higher than that amount plus the factory mileage. (You can Google the distance between the two towns to get an approximation of the miles between the dealerships, using your smart phone.)

Anyway, roughly one fourth of the people who come into the dealership will buy on the first visit, while perhaps one in six will buy at a later time, and a little more than half will buy elsewhere or not buy at all. We had an expression: "Stay with the customer until he buys or dies." A strong salesman will marry you. In fact, he may have no choice. We were obliged by our boss to greet you, and then stay with you from then until you left the lot. If we failed to do that, then we were subject to being fired. If you really just want to look at cars and stickers, you may have to do it when the dealership is closed. Once you come onto the lot, you have a very good chance of buying a car. To the dealer, it's all a numbers game, and you are a number. But if you are made to FEEL like a number, then it is time to find another dealer.

CHAPTER 3:

BUY FROM THE INVOICE

Many dealers advertise that they will show you the actual invoice. If they tell you that you are looking at the invoice, you probably are. You should see the invoice on every car you consider. This will show you the actual dealer cost of the vehicle—with a couple of provisos.

There may be dealer incentives, which will give him more profit than he would normally make. These days, manufacturers may advertise these, so you may know that they exist, but you have to trust the dealer as to the amount, and the first thing you need to learn is to never trust the dealer unless he can show you confirmation. Also, if one manufacturer is advertising "dealer incentives," you may be sure that all manufacturers either have them or are planning to offer them, just to be competitive. You should also try to determine what kind of bonuses are being paid, either by doing an internet search, or by bluffing your sales rep by telling him or her that you know that there are hundreds of dollars in bonus money that don't show up on the invoice. Be very aware that new pricing paradigms may include additional bonuses paid to the dealer that are not at all shown on the invoice. Some of these he may have to earn, but it would be a violation of Federal Fair Trade Laws for the manufacturer to offer bonuses based solely on volume, because smaller dealerships would be unable to compete for those. Nevertheless, there has been a tendency over the past fifty or sixty years for smaller dealerships to fold, and the remaining dealerships to grow larger. The days when a small town like Northfield, Massachusetts, could have two major dealerships, Chevrolet and Ford, with a total population in that area of around 3000 people (and slightly more cows) are long gone. But there are definitely bonuses that are not reflected on the invoice, that the average dealer will qualify for.

The other thing is that the invoice may include a "holdback" or other sum, which is paid back to the dealer after the vehicle is delivered. If you don't know how to read the invoice, you may be unaware of this, but it is usually 3-5% of the invoice amount less the freight charges. To the best of my knowledge, all of the American manufacturers have a holdback on the invoice, and the imports probably do as well. In the old days, it was pretty plainly stated, but now it is not. It may well be hidden in a row or two of figures at the bottom of the invoice, with just initials for identification. There will also be other figures there like an advertising allowance (it may be referred to as a dealer association fee), which the dealer is not paid unless he proves he used the money. But the holdback represents a profit to the dealer that is not a part of the salesman's "commissionable gross profit." In other words, the salesperson is not paid a cent on this part of the dealer's profit. Considering that a well-run back end (the parts and service departments) will pay all of the costs of operating the dealership, before the first car is even sold, this is a bit sinful, but it is in there. The dealer therefore has a built-in profit of several hundred dollars or more on the car, even if he sells it at invoice.

You should also see the invoice to determine what accessories, if any, have been added by the dealership. Dealer installed options are stickered on a separate window sticker also, and the price shown on that sticker is generally five times (5X) what the option cost the dealer. This may not apply to radios, sunroofs, and other things with a high cost for hard parts. But things like "pin striping," rustproofing, paint sealant, and fabric treatments are almost always marked up to 500%, or five times the actual cost to the dealer. In some cases, where the dealer does the installation himself instead of contracting it out, the profit may be even greater than that. This gives the dealer more profit he can negotiate back out of the price. Often the options are not added until the car is ready for delivery. If the option is not physically on the car, you may choose to refuse to pay for it. If it is there, you should offer not more than 25% of the price on the sticker. Radios, sunroofs, extra lights, wheels and tires, "ground effect" kits, and other hardware options may not be marked up quite that much, but will still have at least a 40% profit, and possibly much more. It might be interesting to see, if he has already put a dealer-installed accessory on a particular car, and you did not want it, what would happen if you told him that you wanted to order in another car exactly like it, so you could have it without that option installed. He might just let you have the car with that option, without charging you for it!

Case in point: in 1980, we paid about $35 for the materials and "warranty" for Rusty Jones rustproofing. The lowest-paid kid in the service department (usually the "used car cleanup kid"—my first job in a dealership) did the work, and it costs some money to maintain the service bay, used only for that purpose. The Service Department marked it up for their normal profit, and charged the Sales Department about $80 for rustproofing. We sold it for probably $329 on the sticker. We might have offered it for $229, or even $189 if we wanted the customer to think he was getting a good deal. If the customer really didn't want it, we told the customer that we wanted him to have it, because it would make his car much better at trade-in time, and we wanted him to trade it with us, after all. Then we offered to sell it to him at our cost--$130. This figure was a pure, bald-faced LIE! Very few cars went out without rustproofing. The "warranty" required specific maintenance, including bringing the vehicle into us for a check at specific intervals, so if rust had started, it could be repaired inexpensively. If the customer did not do exactly as the warranty said, the company would refuse to honor the warranty. You will note that I used quotes around the word "warranty," when I first mentioned it above. This is not an actual warranty. All such extended warranties, above what came with the vehicle from the manufacturer, are single-premium insurance policies, and as such carry a very high profit. There may be stipulations such as the one noted on the rustproofing, or there may be a deductible, such that in all but a few cases, you will pay for the greatest portion of the cost of repair. Think of these, not as warranties, but as insurance policies, and determine how much it is worth to you to have that insurance. You might be better off to gamble that you won't have problems. You can also buy towing and rental insurance from your regular insurance agent very cheaply. In that case, the cost of the insurance won't be added to your financed costs. As car loans get longer and longer, the cost of financing such "warranties" gets greater. An extended warranty on drive trains has been offered at times by oil companies and other sources, so you may have other options available for obtaining such coverage. You may well be interested in having an extended warranty on the vehicle, as a means of limiting your costs if there is a problem, but remember that the price of the warranty is negotiable, in most states—though in some states, it must be sold for the full retail price. This might be true, for instance, where such warranties are under control of the state's insurance commissioner, such as Florida. We can't have car dealers competing with insurance agencies, now, can we? The dealer can back some profit from the sale of the warranty out of the car price, however, as long as he shows the warranty at full retail. Note also, however, that rustproofing these days may interfere with the manufacturer's own rust-preventative efforts, such as drains in the bottom of air channels, and so on. If the compound plugs those drains, it might actually increase the likelihood of rust. I doubt that even up north, any dealers still sell that stuff, and I would turn it down in any event, since the manufacturer's warranty now usually contains a rust clause. Another concern along these lines is that the manufacturer's anti-rust warranty is usually stronger, and may be longer, and it gives you more leverage than any aftermarket warranty. You can always scream at the manufacturer, threaten to sue, or whatever. I mention later in the book, that the manufacturers all have customer satisfaction funds, that they can use to satisfy even irrational demands that would cost them more to litigate than to settle, so they will settle a claim even when they know that the customer is in the wrong.

I had a neighbor who recently purchased the extended warranty on his new Ford 4-door pickup truck, since the computer was a $10,000 part, and the warranty was only about $3000. The salesman got him scared that he might actually have to replace the computer. That happens only rarely, however, and usually not until some years have passed. But a low mileage computer might be found in a junkyard from a crashed vehicle, and such a computer will cost considerably less than the dealer retail price of a new computer in the box. If you regularly buy insurance, you may be of the mindset that it is better to pay a little now so that you don't have to pay a lot later if there is a problem with that expensive part. The other side to that equation is that insurance companies are FOR PROFIT companies, and they are making a large profit on that extended warranty. Over the long term, you would most likely be money ahead to avoid the extended warranty. But if the peace of mind is worth more to you than the savings, then go ahead and buy it, but be sure you understand all of the conditions stated in the warranty. And remember that you are paying interest to finance the cost of that warranty throughout the loan period (which may be longer than the warranty coverage period). That could amount to hundreds of dollars, depending on the interest rate and term length, and the price of the warranty. Those warranties frequently contain an opt-out clause, stating that you can have a full refund for up to a year, or something along those lines. Look for that clause before you sign for the warranty, and understand that clause.

Often the dealer will not sell you any of this stuff until after the price is negotiated. If they use a separate F&I guy, he may be the one to offer these warranties, and he will not offer a discount. You may still demand one, however, and they will be happy to sell you the item at a discount, as long as they still make a profit on it. If they use a separate F&I guy, you may be told that you are being turned over to the "Customer Service Manager," or some similar title, "to schedule your delivery." This gets your guard down, and they have a second chance to sell you all of the high-profit dealer retrofit items.

Still, the rule is, "Demand to See the Invoice." Try to get an idea of whether there are factory incentives to the dealer, and if so, try to get an idea of how much they are worth. It could be that the manufacturer is having a contest; with one or two dealers from each region winning a trip to somewhere the owner wants to go for a vacation. If he knows he's close, that may be enough to get him to sell you the car regardless of profit or loss. Who knows? It never hurts to find these out by any way possible. While I would never suggest you buy a car on the internet, it would pay you to try to find the best price you can get on an identical car (with identical options), and then assume that price includes an average markup, and you want the car for less than that! There is no need to tell you the salesperson that you have priced the car online, or what your target may be. Try to determine the amount of any holdback to be paid to the dealer on the car after it is sold. Subtract the amount of any programs or bonuses, and the dealer holdback from the invoice amount to determine the raw cost of the vehicle to the dealer. Now you at least know how to figure how much profit the dealer is actually making on the sale. Add back in the cost of any dealer-installed accessories that you actually want, using the approximations above. Then offer a price that is approximately $100 above the resulting actual cost to the dealer. And finally, hold your guns. Stick to that number. Don't budge unless the dealer lets you walk out the door without signing on the dotted line. If you budge at all, do so in small increments, and not by more than a few hundred dollars total. And NEVER budge by more than the dealer's last gesture. Wear down the dealer. He really wants to sell you that car, and he will do so at ANY profit. And he expects his service department to earn a profit on the car also, which won't happen if he lets you go down the road. There are very few cars that he cannot readily replace on his lot. These days, if you want a Ferrari, or a Mazda Miata, or a Toyota Prius, or whatever the hot selling car is this year, you may have a very small amount of leverage for negotiating, but few other cars are in that category. An electric or hybrid car, or the class mileage leader may be a little tougher to get but that's about it, and with gas prices going down, even those cars are losing their edge.

You should demand to see the invoice as soon as the salesperson asks you for an offer—or as soon as he quotes you the retail figure, preparatory to asking you for an offer.

Just remember that the invoice no longer represents the real cost to the dealership, and while I do not recommend that you purchase a car over the internet, seeing what is the best deal you can get on the car you want, over the internet, will give you the price that you need to beat when you arrive at the dealership you want to buy from, so checking internet prices these days, should be part of your homework before you go looking at cars on the lot at a local dealership. And again, do not tell the dealer that you have been checking prices on the internet, or what prices you have been quoted. He's got lots of secrets he's keeping from you. Let this be one that you keep from him!

I understand that they may have adjusted prices to show a lower profit to dealers since 1995. I have only worked for two dealerships since then, and I don't believe I had access to invoices at either one of those dealerships. (Most dealerships these days don't even want their salespeople to know the actual cost of a vehicle. They try to restrict that information to the management.) If the invoice that they show you indicates less than a 10% profit, then there are incentives that are clearly not shown on the invoice. Assume that the dealer is making at least the 13% figure I discuss in the next paragraph (actual net profit without doing any other calculations), or the 18% figure after you subtract things like freight charges, advertising allowance, and so on. And note that these numbers will not apply to base models or "price leader" models, which actually do have a lower profit margin. There may be bonuses for volume, and also for high customer satisfaction numbers, and for leftover vehicles (called a carryover bonus). In any event, there may be any number of bonuses which the dealer receives—at least some of which he will have to earn—that are not shown on the invoice, so his profit is larger than you may be able to calculate. You can check online for websites which claim to tell you his actual cost, but those I've seen don't seem to do that, and they mostly appear to be from actual dealerships trying to sell you a car. Certainly, you can compare best offers from several dealerships for the same car—but make absolutely certain that the vehicles are, in fact, identical, with exactly the same options. I might suggest that you go out to the dealership at night, and take a photo with your smart phone, of the window sticker on the vehicle you are interested in. Using any regularly available photo editing tool on the smart phone (I like Mobi Systems Photo Suite for Android) black out any identifying information, such as dealer name, dealer number, address, VIN, anything the online dealer could use to track the car down. But by asking him for a price on that specific car, you have a price with the exact same equipment. Also when negotiating with dealerships before you get to the one where you want to buy the car, you may try to offer them extremely low prices, and see if any of them show a spark of interest. That will help you figure out what you should offer your chosen dealership. Any dealer fees are suspect, especially dealer packs for doing registration and title paperwork, which can amount to hundreds or thousands of dollars, where $30 might be closer to the dealer's true cost, and it is a cost of doing business which he should be expected to swallow out of his profit. Floor plan and car prep fees are likewise a cost of doing business, which he should pay out of his profit. If he automatically adds fabric treatment, paint glaze, and rustproofing to the price of all cars, you can refuse to pay any of that, and tell him you don't want any of those things on your car.

I once had a customer who insisted that we made 40% on all cars, and that the invoice we showed him was phony. That was not true then, and probably no dealer would go to the effort of making up a phony invoice. He could go to jail for fraud if he were caught doing that. Average profit for the dealer is closer to 18%, and will vary considerably. For instance, a bottom-end or price leader car will have a profit of perhaps as little as 5% or a few hundred dollars, not counting any holdback or other incentives. As I recall, if you took the bottom-line sticker of a Buick, and subtracted 13%, you would be close to the bottom line of the invoice, with everything added into it. To use the 18% figure, you have to subtract out inland freight, and the advertising allowance, and perhaps some other stuff along those lines, that actually has to be paid to a third party. Of course, after applying the 18% discount, you then have to add back in anything that you subtracted.

If the dealer will not show you the invoice, there are books available on most newsstands which come surprisingly close to the actual invoice cost and "Consumer Reports" (I hate, despise and distrust that magazine and for very good reasons, like I used to sell cameras, and they rated Miranda and Bauer cameras very highly even after they had to report that those models had a very high rate of repair, and took longer to accomplish the repairs than other brands. Funny, but the importer of those brands was located in the same city as the magazine. Then a photography magazine caught them using wide angle lenses to make the trunks of American cars look larger than imports, which were always shot with longer focal-length lenses, thus distorting any difference in size. Hence, I believe I cannot trust that magazine.) But CR does publish an annual Automobile issue, in which they publish a percentage number that will allow you to come very close to the dealer's actual invoice total, using a calculator. In fact, if you carry a smart phone into the dealership, you can use it to search for a website that publishes such information. And you can use your phone as well, to do financial calculations, so that you can, for instance, double-check any interest figures the Finance Manager gives you. Given a cost, a time period for payback, and an interest rate, you can sit there on your smart phone and know the exact monthly payment to the penny. Someone in your party should always have a smart phone, and be ready to whip it out with no hesitation, and know how to use it to find car prices and other information. If the dealer sees you checking up on him, you may be surprised at how honest he can become. I like to use "Financial Calculators" by Bishinews (www.fncalculator.com) on my Windows and Android phones and tablets, for this purpose, but there are any number of apps available for any phone or tablet system you may own.

In order to figure the exact percentage of profit the way the industry does, you must subtract things like inland freight, do your profit calculations, and then add back the things you subtracted. The 13% figure I used above was determined without doing all of that, and was an average based on the price at the bottom at the bottom of the manufacturer's window sticker. As a quick and dirty figure, it was about as close as you could get, but you should try to get closer than that if you can. And remember that price leader models will always be lower, and real luxury liners will likely be higher. Use that figure only as a last resort, and bear in mind that it might not be applicable to all brands. You should have these guidelines available from any source, but they are at best a poor substitute for seeing the actual invoice. One of the best sources in the past has been the quarterly edition of the NADA (National Auto Dealers Association) Auto Price Guide. This is an extremely useful tool for determining the value of used cars, such as the one you are trading, or possibly might be trying to buy, but the Quarterly edition, which is much larger than the monthly one, publishes, or used to, actual dealer cost figures on new cars. Their website, http://www.nadaguides.com is also a valuable resource to have loaded in your browser on the first tab, before you head for the dealership. I also like Edmund's website www.edmunds.com, and there are others like www.kbb.com by Kelly Blue Book, which you might like to look at before you go shopping. You can also Google "New car dealer invoice cost" or words to that effect, and come up with other sources for of this information. Be aware that most of those responses will be out-of-town dealers wanting to sell you a new car. They can truck it to you, or arrange to have you pick it up at your local dealer's location.

After the paperwork is signed, is no time to be asking for any kind of discount on any part of the deal. Once the papers are signed, you are committed to the deal as it was written down. You might be able to back out of it if you could prove it was fraudulent, or something like that, but it could cost you a fortune in legal fees. We had a Toyota Celica ST coupe for sale—a nice bright, Forest Green one, which NOBODY wanted. The thing had been sitting in our showroom for simply ages, and we would have happily given the thing away for our pure cost. A girl who was a friend of someone who had bought a used car from me came in, and just loved that car. (Well, there's no accounting for taste, is there?) Actually, I could have lived with it myself, but who would dare say so, when everyone else hated it? It had a nice beige interior, and we had had our pin-stripe contractor put some bold beige stripes on the outside, to tie it to the interior. The girl came to see me, as she had promised she would when her friend picked up her used car, and she quickly signed the papers on that green Celica ST coupe. After it was all inked in, at full retail, and she was walking out of the showroom, she asked me "I don't suppose that there's any such thing as a discount on Toyotas...." Of course, I replied that there certainly was not, since we couldn't keep them in stock, due to the gas crunch, and Toyota's outstanding reputation for reliability. And I laughed all the way to the bank.

Buying from the invoice is one step which can save you hundreds or thousands of dollars just by itself, when you know how to do it. You should NEVER buy a new car without seeing the invoice. If you don't see the invoice, the dealer knows everything, and you know nothing. You are blind. But these days, even if you see the invoice, you are not getting all the information available. Don't even think of buying a car without seeing the invoice. There are enough dealers out there who will OFFER to show it to you, that any dealer should be willing to do so on request. But remember that invoice minus the holdback is almost certainly not the bottom line anymore. The dealer is almost certain to have additional profits that do not show up on the invoice.

CHAPTER 4:

THE QUOTA SYSTEM

Dealers have a monthly quota system. This can work a little differently, depending on whether the model is very hot in the marketplace, or whether it is a real turkey, and they force him to take more than he could possibly sell. Sometimes, a dealer may use this to his advantage in swapping cars with another dealership. If my dealership has a red IROC Camaro in stock, and another dealer's customer just can't live without that car, but we also have six Chevy Suburbans that we can't move, we might be willing to swap the red IROC if the other dealer were willing to take two of the Suburbans off our hands. This sort of wheeling and dealing goes on all of the time.

The manufacturer may also have a deal whereby you can get one really hot model for every fifty cars you sell, and you want to sell at least fifty cars each month, so you can get the one you want each month. Larger dealers will want to work up to the next multiple of fifty cars each month, so if they are close to a multiple of fifty units (or whatever the breaking point is), they are much more willing to deal on any vehicle in their inventory.

With slow sellers, the quota system simply means that you get so many of the slow sellers each month, period. That means you will get so many more next month, whether or not you sell the ones you got this month. This means that as the month draws to a close, and you are sitting on a number of slow movers, you are getting anxious to move them.

But what about the fast movers? There is a double whammy there. Toyota once dropped our monthly allocation of two Tercels on our lot very late in the month—about the 27th or so. We had a dozen orders written for Tercels. The white one went out right away to a customer who had written an order for just that car. The other one was light metallic blue, which at the time was Toyota's most popular color. But none of our customers would touch the car! It was incredible. We put it on the front line and it sold within 45 minutes. But for a time, there, we were very scared that we were going to be sitting on the car after the month had been closed out.

What effect would that have had? Well, Toyota had allocated us two Tercels per month. But last month we got two, and only sold one of them. So this month they would only allocate us one Tercel. Worse yet, since we had one Tercel still on the lot from last month, they would count that as our allocation for this month, and not ship us ANY Tercels. A dealer who does not make his quota on a fast selling model is in big trouble.

How does that affect the buyer? Well, first of all, no matter what car you want to buy, it means that there is one time of the month that is better than any other time. You should make sure before you get to the dealership that you can finance the new car. Check with your own bank (or Credit Union) and make sure that they will finance the car for you. If they won't, the dealer may still be able to get you financed, since it is common for the dealer to sign a "recourse" agreement with his financing partners, which means that the dealer will buy the car and pay off the note if the bank has to repossess it. That means that the bank (or other finance company) can't lose any money on the deal, and so the bank will be more likely to go for it than if you walked in on your own.

Anyway, what you want is the ability to close the deal quickly. Walk into the dealership about 48-60 hours before the end of the business month. At that point, anything on the dealer's lot that is not yet sold, the dealer is getting anxious to move. This means that he is most anxious to talk to you, and will be willing to let you make the terms. The salesman also has a quota to fill. If he is below his quota, he will be more willing to work to sell you a car for no commission—or for the so-called "flat fifty" that they will pay him for moving a vehicle. (All right, thanks to inflation, that may be more like a flat hundred these days....)

Sometimes the dealer will hold the books open on a month past the end of the month, so he might even be able to close off a car that was sold on the 31st of the month, so don't hesitate to be even later than 48-60 hours before the close of business on the last working day of the month. You want to get there when the dealer really has ants in his pants. Of course, to get the best deal, you have to take something that is on the lot, or something that he can swap for, with another nearby dealer, very quickly. If you are looking for a hot seller, you could get lucky and find one somewhere, and still be able to get a good deal on it, if you are not picky about color choice and options— and a large number of options can be dealer installed, so you may still have a chance to get your choice there.

If the car you want is a total toad, and the dealer has lots of them in stock, don't even hesitate to offer him a deal that would be an actual loss for him. He might take it if you stick to your guns. He wants that thing out of there.

If what you are looking for is an average mover, he still will be more interested in moving it especially if he is close to some particular breaking point in his quota system. In any event, if there is no particular limit on that model, he can easily replace the car the following month—and both the salesman and the dealer principal want to have the best possible numbers for the end of the month.

We should also note that the best particular month to buy a new car is December. Nobody buys cars in December. The dealer is more anxious to talk to you then, and you will get more attention from the salesman then. July is also pretty slow. The very worst time to buy a car is Washington's Birthday Weekend, when every sucker in P. T. Barnum's date book is lining the lots with cash in hand ready to buy at any price the dealer throws out, convinced that they bought during a "sale," and hence got a good deal.

Similarly, don't be too impressed with advertised sales. Another bad time to buy may well be one of those deals where a number of dealers get together and put up a mass display in a local football stadium, or mall parking lot. Those places are a madhouse! You might be well advised to look and compare then, but do not buy a car then. Again, at those times, the lot is lined with suckers who all have "buying fever," and will buy at any price the dealer throws out. That sort of fever is catching, and you do not want to catch it.

Buy your car the last possible day of the month, and during one of the slower months of the year. The only possible exception would be if your wanted to buy one of last year's models with factory cash all around, in which case you buy near the close of the last month you think you can still find the car you want. And remember that the car will automatically be worth less in trade— possibly by an amount as large or larger than the amount you saved by taking last year's model now. My father was once offered the choice of which year he wanted his Renault titled as. That was back when they were retitling cars for the new year when they stayed on the dealer lots, and there were no model year differences. (Honda was once sued for doing that with some of their motorcycles, and now they don't do that sort of thing anymore. The idiots who sued Honda cost themselves and me many times the value of the settlement, in lost trade-in value, when Honda dumped the old models on the market for very attractive prices. Some people never know when to leave well enough alone, I swear…. But of course, the lawyers made lots of money, and that is what drives suits like that one.) Since 1980, the VIN on every vehicle sold in the USA contains a year code, the tenth digit in the 17-digit VIN. Anyway, because Massachusetts had an excise tax on cars, my father chose to take it with the older title, because there was a tax savings, and he also considered the fact that he drove 40,000 miles a year, and 80,000 miles wouldn't look as bad on a three-year-old car as it would on a two-year-old one, or affect its trade-in value as much. These kinds of factors may still influence your decision in that area. If there is a major change in the body style, you will want to weigh the decision more carefully than if there are no external differences. The new body style will hold its value better than the older one. On the other hand, there are those who feel that the new models may have some bugs that weren't ironed out in development.

My choice would be for the newer style, but that is a personal decision, which is yours to make, and to live with.

Another thing you might look for, especially if you are interested in a slow mover, is the date the car was shipped to the dealer. Dealers don't generally own the vehicles on their lot. The vehicles are financed under what is called a "Floor Plan Agreement." The dealer pays interest only (he makes no principal payments) on the cars. There is one exception to this. If the car sits around for a long time, the bank wants some of the principal on that car paid off. This is usually done in 90-day increments, and if the car has been there for a year, the bank may well want the whole principal amount paid off. I am told that this sort of agreement is less common now than it used to be. The dealer would have to really love the car to want to pay it off, and generally he doesn't love anything on the lot that much. Still, older cars have cost him more than they are worth in interest payments. If the car you are looking at has been around for a time approaching a multitude of 90 days, the dealer may be more anxious to move that car, even at a loss. There may also be a similar model to what you want, but in a different color or something, which falls into that category, and if you are willing to take the older car, the dealer will be more willing to talk to you.

In a time of fast price hikes, you may also get a lower sticker price on an older unit. I went looking for a Japanese pickup truck in 1979. I wound up finding a yellow Dodge D-50 Sport, made by Mitsubishi, which had been in stock long enough so that there was a $220 discount for no radio and no bed light, which were coming as standard equipment on new units, and in the meantime the new units had a $300 increase in the retail sticker price. The combination made this particular truck over $500 less expensive than vehicles that had arrived since that one did, even without a discount. I told the dealer I wanted to think about it (I knew where there was another one just like it) and he called me a couple of days later to offer me an extra $200 on my trade-in, which was an old Mercury Capri that I had bought after some idiot totaled my wagon. I signed the deal, with a discount, an over-allowance, and the reduced sticker price. I could not have touched anything comparable at the time for anywhere near the price. Before I found the Dodge, I had heard good things about the Toyota, and had been unhappy with a previous Datsun, so I went to a Toyota dealer and test drove the pickup, which was at a lower trim level than the Dodge, but far more expensive. I had told the salesman there that I wanted to look at other brands, and shop prices before buying. I fell in love with that truck. It handled much better than the Dodge, was obviously built better than the Datsun, and I wanted to drive out of there in that truck, I just did not let the dealer know that. I asked him how much I could buy it for that day, and he threw me a price of $4300 or so. It was low enough that I knew it was a good deal, especially since it was the long-bed Deluxe model, not a base truck. But he had heard what I had said earlier about shopping around. I whipped out my checkbook and told him to write it up. You should have seen him back-pedal. He would not sell me the truck. The other Toyota dealer I checked with wanted much more money for a truck with the same specs. After I bought the Dodge, I wound up accepting a position as a Toyota salesman for the second Toyota dealer, and learned that the first dealer was well known for a technique called "low-balling," in which the dealer quotes you a price for which he knows that absolutely no other dealer will sell you that vehicle. When you are done shopping, you will come back to him. At that time, he will refuse to honor the price he quoted, but you already know the next-best price you were quoted, and all he thinks he has to do to sell you the vehicle is to beat that price.

The technique occasionally works, but it can also lead to a very loud scene, such as I threw at the time, and possibly consumer complaints to the authorities, or even a class-action lawsuit. If a dealer low-balls you, you should absolutely refuse to buy from him under any circumstances, and don't hesitate to make your experience known. You will need a witness, should you decide to complain to the authorities. I squawked loudly enough at that time that every other customer in the shop heard me loud and clear!

Another technique which falls into my "Do not buy from this dealer under any circumstances," category, is any entry on a dealer sticker, of a price increase due to "market availability," or anything similar. This means that during a gas crunch, if you are looking at a small car, the dealer may raise the price by hundreds of dollars, just because the car is in high demand. This is gouging, pure and simple, and I would find another dealer, pronto. Even if the dealer offered to discount the added price, I would prefer to deal with someone who marked the car honestly, and refused to discount it. I would expect that dealer to be more honest after the sale as well.

So, there are ways that you can use the quota system to your advantage. The biggest thing is to shop very near the end of the month. Picking the right month may also help. And if you find a car that has been on the lot for a period approaching a multiple of 90 days, you may be able to get the best deal on that car, or any car, which has been there a long time.

CHAPTER 5:

GETTING THE RIGHT

TRADE-IN ALLOWANCE

Most people do not pay cash for their new car. They trade an older car. This gives the dealer one more area for profit. Do you know what your trade is really worth? How does a dealer determine what the trade is worth? Does it matter whether you deal on the new car before you discuss the vehicle you are trading in?

Your used car has a value, which you can easily establish. This is called its "Actual Cash Value," or "ACV," in dealer-speak. This is the wholesale value of your used car— what the used car dealer down the street would be willing to pay him for it. There are a couple of ways you can determine this value. If you have a friendly banker, he will show you his NADA used car value guide (or whatever book he uses to value used cars.) The value of a clean car, which does not need any work at all, is the "bank loan" value. Forget the retail, trade, and wholesale columns. From that figure, subtract the high mileage adjustment where applicable—but do not add anything for low mileage. I never said these guys were fair....

Now subtract the full retail value of any repairs needed, replacement of any worn tires, and so on. If the car is dirty, the upholstery torn, or whatever, you need to subtract the full retail value of bringing it up to par. Any parts, such as tires, that the car needs, should be comparable to what was on the car when it left the factory as a new car. The figure you get after all that subtracting is the Actual Cash Value of your car.

Another way to determine this is to simply approach several used car dealers and ask what they would pay you for the car, in cash. If they want the car, they won't lowball you, since you could sell it to anyone, and they know it. Ask enough dealers, and you will get a good sense of the ACV of your car. If one dealer is really hot to trot, see if he will give you a written promise to buy the car for that price.

Now when you go shopping, get the lowest possible price on the new car first, before you discuss trade. You might tell the dealer you will be giving the trade to a relative or whatever. When you have the deal you want on the new car, ask the dealer to appraise your trade-in. If he offers you more than you determined that your car was worth, sign quickly. If he offers you less, ask him to justify his price. If you have a firm offer from a used car dealer, inform the new car dealer of this. The used car dealer will pay the same price to the new car dealer that he would have paid you, and that becomes the trade-in value. Often, if a new car dealer is trying to put together a deal with you, and he can't offer what you want in trade, he will ask you to leave the car with him for a day so that he can "shop" it around to used car dealers. This simply means that if he can find a used car dealer willing to pay him more than he thought it was worth, that value becomes the allowance. You can do this before you even get to the new car dealer, and it will put you in a better position to dicker with him on the new car.

You should do this anyway, because the dealer might low-ball you on the trade, or might not want your trade at all, and so will offer you well below its true wholesale value. If you go in there with an inflated idea of your trade's value, you might walk out in a huff, when the dealer offered you a fair trade-in allowance. If you have chewed him down on the new car, there is no room for a mistake on your trade-in.

This transaction is really two car deals. You buy the new car from the dealer at retail, and he buys the used one from you at wholesale. You are entitled to chew him down as far as possible on the new one, and to get every penny of the ACV for the used one, but no more. Sometimes a dealer makes a mistake on the used car, and has to eat the thing, or take a major loss.

Once I took in an Oldsmobile Custom Cruiser, which showed high miles on it. The trader insisted that the miles were original. We later discovered signs that there were at least a hundred thousand more miles than what showed (and maybe two hundred thousand!) We lost our shirt on that one. On the other hand, a guy came in one time with an old Corolla that was badly rusted. My boss said "this guy is a first-generation immigrant, and they fight you for the last penny," and he sent me out with a trade-in value (against full retail on the new Celica) of $700. The boss told me to work the customer very hard, because of the rust and such, but don't let him walk out, because we had room to move. I told the customer that his car was very rusty, and we couldn't pay too much for it, then I hit him with the figures. He said "Okay," and I wrote the deal. My boss was flabbergasted. ACV on the trade was $1500. We had just made an extra $800 on the deal. Had the customer known his ACV, we could not have done that!

Could you do better selling your car privately? If you can get quick cash for the car, there are a couple of things you need to bear in mind. In states with sales tax, most of the time, the sales tax is paid only on the trade difference. Thus, as a trade, your car is worth to you, the Actual Cash Value PLUS the amount of your sales tax on that amount. If your neighbor can pay you quick cash in an amount greater than ACV plus the sales tax on the ACV, then you are better off financially to sell to your neighbor. You are NOT better off to sell to a used car dealer for ACV, since then you will pay sales tax on the full purchase price of the new car. And remember, time is of the essence, since you are trying to put together the whole deal in the last couple of days of the month. Your banker (and your neighbor's banker) would have to be very friendly to accommodate you in an unnecessarily complicated deal like that. Since your neighbor will probably be getting the car cheaper than he could buy it at retail from the used car dealer, he might be anxious to split the difference with you, but generally, the convenience of trading is worth the difference—and remember, if you trade it to a dealer, you don't have to warranty it. If your neighbor buys it from you, and it blows up the next week, many states will force you to do the repairs. (You are subject to the implied warranty provisions and suitability for its intended use, of the Uniform Commercial Code.) Generally speaking, you would be better off to trade. If your neighbor still wants the car, take him to your salesman, and let the neighbor strike a deal on the used car before you actually trade it. That way, your neighbor will get the best deal, since the dealer doesn't lay out any money for the used car (which is rarely floor-planned) and the dealer has to warranty the car to the neighbor. Your neighbor pays the sales tax on his purchase either way, and you avoid the sales tax on the ACV of your trade. PLUS, you might even get your salesman to pay you a bird-dog on the used car deal!

If you don't have a ready buyer for the car, then you will have to pay advertising costs, and have to wait to sell it. You will also have to contend with every Tom, Dick, and Harry who will want to test drive it (they are under no obligation to buy it if they crunch it) and who may want you to take back financing for at least part of the price. Trading is MUCH easier than that! You just drive to the dealership in your old car, and drive home in the new one.

And speaking of sales tax, if you buy your car across the state line, from a dealer in another state, sales tax will be charged at the rate applicable at your home, or the principal place of garaging. Sales tax is paid at the time of registration. Normally, the dealer is required to handle the registration for you. At one point, I recall that a group of gay men in Rhode Island complained that Rhode Island wasn't doing enough for gay people, and so they were going to buy everything in Massachusetts, so that Rhode Island would lose sales tax revenues. Those guys said that in the case of major purchases like cars, the state would lose a significant amount of money. Such a statement was pure ignorance. The governor probably laughed all the way to the bank, carrying the sales tax revenue from their newly purchased cars. DO NOT think that you can save a per-cent or two on sales tax by purchasing in a neighboring state with a lower sales tax rate. Ditto for a neighboring county or municipality. Tax is paid at the rate prevailing at the address on the registration. (If you can legitimately register it elsewhere, and get away with it, you may be able to save tax that way, but if you get caught, you could be arrested for tax fraud. For instance, if you have a vacation home in another state, and register it there, but park it at your principal home most of the year, the tax should be paid at the principal place of garaging, which would be your full-time home, not your vacation cottage.)

And generally speaking, while the dealer will subtract the full retail value of any needed repairs from the bank loan value, to obtain the ACV, you would NOT be advised to do the repairs first. The exception would be where you can get the repairs done for much less than the retail value of that repair. For instance, if the car is running rough, and you know that the high high-tension leads need replacement, you might do that, for $20 or so if you do it yourself, and then the dealer won't knock off $120 for a tune-up. If your seat is torn, and a local salvage yard has the exact same seat, same fabric and color, for $20, you might swap seats, and save the $60 the dealer will charge for sewing the seat. If the paint is faded, and a quick polish will fix it, you could save hundreds of dollars he might mark it down for a paint job. But don't pay full price to have repairs done, just to raise the ACV by what you paid for the repairs. I can buy good used tires for under $20 each, and change them for free. That beats a deduction of $80 each for worn tires. But make sure that the tires you buy are good enough to avoid the deduction from ACV. If you are not certain it will save you money, don't bother with the repair.

You are dealing in empirical figures when you buy a car. The new car has a fixed cost, and the Actual Cash Value of your trade, while it may vary a few dollars, depending on how badly the dealer wants it, is reasonably fixed. If you don't have a really good idea of BOTH of those figures, the dealer has two chances to make a profit on you. The more accurately you know those figures, the tighter you can force the dealer to deal, and that means money in your pocket. And don't forget the effect of sales tax in your calculations.

CHAPTER 6:

FINANCING THE
PURCHASE

We have already talked a bit about the dealer's F&I guy, and how the dealer usually has a "recourse" agreement with at least one of his finance sources. But is there any savings available to you in financing through a dealer? The answer to that is "maybe."

The dealer will insist that you buy credit life insurance on the note, and that will cost you more through the dealer than through your own bank. Therefore, if the interest rates quoted are the same, your own bank may offer you lower payments.

Dealers can finance through several banks, and they generally get a rebate of several per-cent on the finance rate. Some of that is for handling the paperwork, and some of it is for doing volume business, and some of it may come from signing recourse agreements.

Generally speaking, though, the dealer will get about 3 to 4% off the going rate on a new car loan, (that was true when interest rates were around ten per cent, so figure accordingly when rates are lower) and lower amounts off the rate on used car loans, with the amount diminishing as the car gets older. The dealer's rebate may vary, of course, with the interest prevailing at the time. It probably will not drop below 3% if interest rates are close to the double-digit point, but at the time of this writing interest rates are at an all-time low, so he might not even get a full one per cent.

When the dealer asks you to finance with him, tell him your own banker will give you the same rate, and you feel more comfortable dealing with your own banker. Don't close the door fully, however, if you don't already have a banker in mind. Tell the dealer rep that if he can offer you a significantly better rate, you will consider financing through him. That should open the floodgates. You want him to give you at least 1% off the going rate. When he gives you the best rate you think you can get from him, it's time to compare actual payments. Your own banker may still be lower, because of the difference in credit life insurance. You might check with your own insurance agent, as well, to see if (s)he can write you an acceptable credit life insurance policy at a lower cost than the dealer's policy. Another choice here might be a declining value policy that would pay off the note, but not repair the vehicle or give you anything for your equity, IF your object here is to achieve the lowest possible financing cost. When interest rates are high, the interest on the loan could easily amount to thousands of dollars over the life of the loan. If you carry a smart phone or tablet, you can download financial calculators that will allow you to perform what-if comparisons of different loan rates right on your phone. If not, you can get a financial calculator for under $40 at Radio Shack or any office supply store. With such a tool, you can compute payments, and get an idea of the savings possible by substituting different financial parameters. When I first started selling cars, our F&I guy had a desktop calculator that cost at least $2000, to do these computations. You could not have afforded to keep up with him, and you would have had to have a very friendly banker to do them on his calculator for you. Now there is no excuse not to have the means with you when you walk into the dealership, to check up on the F&I guy's work. If you use such a tool in front of the dealer rep, he will see that he can't pull the wool over your eyes as easily as he can with most customers. Make sure that you are very comfortable using your financial calculator or app, before you go into the dealership. Spending some time discussing these things with your friendly banker before you go to the dealership will also arm you with more information on the different ways to proceed with financing.

If you don't have a personal banker, most newspapers publish local bank loan rates. If a bank has a lot of money it wants to loan out for short term notes, it may offer a considerably better rate than other banks in the area for car loans, which are a secured, short term loan. Instead of quoting your own banker's rates to the dealer, you might wish to quote such a bank's published rates.

If the dealer offers an insurance package, this is a profit center for the dealership, and is subject to price negotiation. Check with your own insurance agent to find out prices on all the coverages you require, and be armed with this information when you visit the dealer. The dealer is probably not going to be willing to beat your agent's prices, but he might, so it is worth looking into. And the dealer might offer a declining balance collision policy, which might pay off the balance if the car were totaled, but not pay for the repairs if they were more than the remaining principle amount. Such a policy offers you less protection than full collision coverage, but at a lower cost, and might be worth considering.

Remember that the cost of any dealer insurance is added to the principal amount financed, and you pay finance charges on it for the life of the loan. That can get expensive, so figure your insurance charges through the dealer as the difference in payment with and without the insurance, then compare with your agent's rates. You should also be sure that the insurance company is a reputable one. A hole-in-the-wall insurance company could refuse to pay a claim, and then you are liable for the amount of the damages—and in some cases that amount could be trebled for the refusal to pay. You should check on the actual company no matter where you buy your insurance— and the agents who advertise that they can furnish insurance regardless of previous cancellations are the worst in that regard. Once an agent wrote my compulsory policy through a major insurer, and then wrote the property damage policy with a hole-in-the-wall insurance company, which resulted in a lawsuit being filed against me. No thanks, stick with reputable agents and companies. Some states may not permit car dealers to sell insurance at all.

The dealerships I have worked for have been strict about obeying laws regarding credit and credit checks. There are a number of dealers out there who will obtain your Social Security number at the earliest opportunity, and run a credit check on you.

There are a couple of reasons for this. For one thing, it tells him whether you can buy a car or not. He knows if you are upside down on your trade (which means that you owe more than the ACV) and whether his bank will approve your credit application.

Another technique is called "poisoning the water." If there are a lot of requests for credit information in a short period of time, banks assume that the other lenders turned you down. A dealer might even pull several credit checks on you over a two or three-day period, to give banks the impression that he was waiting for something to be removed from the file before he submitted it. That dealer will have an explanation for those credit checks, but no other dealer will. Banks who received the application first will have a credit file that doesn't show the extra checks, but new banks will see all of those credit checks, and assume that something is wrong. Bankers are suspicious, and will turn down an application just because of a large number of inquiries on your credit bureau file. What other reason would he have for asking for your Social Security number? Perhaps you just misunderstood…. Don't give anyone your Social Security number unless and until you are interested in listening to what kind of credit deal the dealer can arrange for you! Recently I was in the market for a motorcycle, and I approached a dealer who submitted my application to a very large number of finance companies, each of which ran a credit check on me. That lowered my credit score instantly, and he got only one approval, and it required a down payment equal to more than I wound up paying for the bike I bought! Needless to say, I will not be buying any motorcycles from that dealer anytime soon. When I was selling motorcycles, we ran the credit bureau report ourselves, and then faxed it to the finance companies along with the credit application. That way, only one credit report was run on that customer as a result of our application process. What this guy did to me would never have happened to our customers! If something like this happens to you at a particular dealership, write the credit bureaus, and see if they will restore your credit score to where it was. Note that all three bureaus issue different scores for the same person, as well, because they rank things differently. TransUnion gives me a vastly higher score than Experian, for instance. If any dealer does anything which results in a lowering of your credit score, even temporarily, you should file a complaint with the consumer protection authorities in your state, and inform everyone you know that they should avoid that dealership at all costs!

The dealer may ask to see your driver's license before a test drive, but if he copies the number down, in states where it is the same as your Social Security number, you can expect him to run a credit check. (I believe all states should have stopped that situation by now, because it makes your SS number too public, and the Feds frown on that.) My first impression is that you simply do not want to do business with this kind of dealer, and rather than giving him the number, get off his lot and find someplace else to buy your car. This is especially true if you phone the dealer first, and he wants this information over the phone. He has NO legitimate reason to obtain this information until he has a deal and is ready to talk financing. Likewise, you should not bring up the subject of financing until the deal is struck. If you have questions about financing before you shop for a car, visit a banker or a Credit Union loan officer, and ask him. Note that I said a banker, not a finance company. Bankers usually play straight with you, and they usually abide by the law. (I once had a banker tell a friend of his that a piece of property I was trying to buy was for sale, and the friend made a higher offer than I had, so this is certainly not always true.) With car dealers and "mouse houses" (the term comes from a popular Walt Disney character whose name in general use is not consistent with the quality with which Disney would like to be associated) you cannot be sure that they will abide by the law. If you bring up the subject of financing with the dealer before the deal is struck, you allow him to play fast and loose with you.

How about financing versus paying cash for the car? Finance interest is paid on a declining balance. Interest on savings is earned on a steady basis if you collect and spend the interest, and on an increasing balance if you reinvest the interest. In either case, if you finance the car, you will have the cash in the bank when the car is paid for. If you pay cash, you will NOT have the money in the bank when the car is paid for, and unless you actually pay YOURSELF back for the loan, you will be forever out that cash. You are therefore generally better off to finance the car. I can remember my father computing the difference once, to see whether he would be better off financing or paying cash—but he only compared the interest for the time of the loan, and did not consider the interest on the savings if he still had the money in the bank.

On ten thousand dollars, over five years, at 6% interest earned on savings, versus 12 per cent loan interest, the interest paid on the loan would be $3,346.67, while the interest earned on savings, if reinvested, would be $3,488.50—at half the interest rate—and you still have the money in the bank! If you took the interest out, with monthly compounding (as all of these were figured) you would have $50.00 each month to help make the car payments of $222.44 per month, or you would earn and spend $4,000.00 over the life of the loan. There might be circumstances here where you might want to pay cash for the car, but I can't imagine what they would be. It might be interesting to see what would happen if you took a shorter-term loan, and took the cash out in a few large sums, and see how you come out. But if you are capable of leaving the interest in to compound, while making the payments, you will be money ahead at the end of five years. If you invest your savings in a mutual fund that averages about a 27% gain every year, the savings will actually make the car payments for you— and you will STILL have the principal amount in your savings when the car is paid for. Such investments usually bear closer scrutiny than fully insured savings accounts, but there are certainly funds out there that have this kind of return. If you invest the money at 27%, and leave the gains in there to reinvest, your $10,000.00 will be worth $38,001.35 after five years. Note that with interest rates down now, you would not have to earn that 27% to pay for the car. Assuming ten thousand dollars for 6 years at 3% interest on the loan, earning 12% annually would leave more in the mutual fund than the total you paid for the car, and just over 1.5% per month would give you enough to make the payments, and that would be about 19% per year, and that is if you took out the interest every month to make the payments. These kinds of earnings are readily available if you have that kind of money to invest, so paying cash for a car would seem to make no sense at all!

There are a lot of options when it comes to financing, but in general, paying cash for a car is not the way to go, unless you have those earnings every year, and nothing else to spend them on. Just make sure that you get the possible deal on the financing. No sense in lining other people's pockets with your money.

Just as I was getting ready to publish this book, I saw news accounts of a bill in Congress, which would potentially remove existing regulations to protect minorities from discrimination in financing new cars. Dealerships mark up the cost of finance, and can add additional costs to the sales price of the vehicle, in anticipation that the finance company might charge minorities a higher rate. Current regulations prohibit this, but the auto dealers own the Congress, so they are trying to change those regulations. Keep aware of ongoing news on this issue. If that bill passes, and is not vetoed, and if you are Black, or Hispanic, or possibly female, or very old, or so young that you don't have much credit established or if you walk into the dealership with a same-sex partner, you could pay much higher financing charges than if you do not fall into a minority category. If this bill passes, and you think you might be affected by it, you should establish a very good relationship with a Credit Union, or possibly a local bank, before you even think about shopping for a car!

The cost of financing your new car purchase can run to thousands of dollars. There is a potential for saving hundreds of dollars on the financing. The dealer's interest rate is as negotiable as the price on the window sticker. Take advantage of that fact, and don't fail to do your financial homework before you go in to see the dealer.

Interest rates have come down lately, but the techniques discussed here still apply. And while I have not dealt with them specifically here, Credit Unions are likely to be better than an actual bank, and they should certainly be one of the places where you shop as well. They are owned by the people who bank there, and so they tend to be more friendly in setting policies than other financial institutions. For instance, I get any checks that are direct-deposited into my credit union, one day faster, in general, than I would get the money from that check credited to my account in a bank.

CHAPTER 7:

BUYING A USED CAR

While this book is primarily aimed at saving the new car buyer money, these same tips can be used to save money on used cars as well. The dealer cost of a used car can be determined as shown in the chapter on getting the right trade-in allowance. Markups on used cars are higher than on new cars, and many salesmen at new car dealerships prefer to sell used cars, since the commissions are higher. If you are a strong negotiator, you can save a lot of money on used cars.

Used car are not floor-planned, so the dealer has his own money tied up in them. For that reason, he generally wants to move them out quickly. He will wholesale anything he doesn't think that he can move profitably, to a used car dealer. He does this for a couple of reasons. For one thing, he gets his money quickly that way. For another thing, he doesn't have to worry about a warranty.

A few new car dealers will let you look at their "auction line" and choose a car for little more than what he would wholesale the car for. This practice has fallen off in states with strong consumer protection laws. One thing to look for is a late model that looks good, but has high miles on it. It is nothing these days to see a car go 200,000 miles without major problems. The high-miles car probably has been well maintained, and most of its miles were probably put on while driving over the Interstate Highway system, which is an easy life for most modern cars. It is usually capable of giving very good service for several more years, yet the price will be extremely attractive.

In 1985, I bought a 1982 GMC S-15 pickup from a local Ford dealer who had not been able to move it for four months. He reportedly had turned down $3000 from another dealer when he first took it in trade, yet he sold it to me for $2500. I test drove it, and thought it was almost as tight as when it was new. It had plenty of pep. The tires had good tread, but were smaller than what the manufacturer called for. I later bought spoked rims and four "blemished" Firestone tires for $300 installed and balanced. These were oversized tires which looked good and worked well on the truck. The truck had 83,000 miles on it when I bought it: nobody wanted it with that many miles on it. I paid cash, and later borrowed $3000 against it, and when I couldn't pay the note, the bank repossessed it. I had owned it nearly three years, and put 43,000 miles on it, during which time the only major repair was a clutch and then a flywheel, which should have been replaced with the clutch. I had rebuilt the alternator and put in a battery, and taken one tube out of the radiator. That was it. The bank wanted more than $2500 to redeem it, and I told them that if it was worth that much to them, they'd better keep it. I figured the ACV at $1500. I got really good use out of it, and my actual cost per mile was very low, thanks to the bank, which effectively "bought" it from me for more than I had paid for it. Of course, it did damage my credit score....

If you are looking at a used car, here's a tip that's worth well more than the price of this book. I don't care if it's the middle of summer and it's a hundred and ten degrees in the shade, and the air conditioning on this piece of crap you're test driving doesn't even work, CHECK THE HEATER!!!! You need to do this for two reasons: first, if the heater core is bad, the part is about $100 on most cars, even more from the dealer, of course, but the labor is an all-day job for a competent mechanic with the right tools, so you will pay in excess of $600 labor to exchange the heater core, because the whole dashboard has to come apart! And the second reason is a little more obtuse, but indicates at least a possibility of even more serious damage. The only thing I know of that regularly plugs a heater core, is block sealer. A non-working heater is a sign that someone may have used block sealer on this vehicle at some time in the past. It may be your sleazy dealer, or he may have bought the car at auction from someone even more sleazy than himself, and he wasn't even aware of the heater problem, or it may be that some new-car customer put a can of block sealer into this piece of crap so he could keep the new car dealer's appraisers from discovering that it had a cracked head. All of that does not matter. If the heater does not work, I don't care how much you think you love this car, it is not worth the hassles, and the kinds of problems it could be telling you about are those that might show up long after any warranty on the car is used up. I once met a woman who had a total engine failure almost immediately (I discuss this in the warranty section) and the warranty company refused to cover the repair because they said that she had run the car without coolant. When she first turned on the heater the next winter, there was no heat. Her (long-time, trusted) mechanic attempted to clear the blockage by flushing AND reverse flushing the cooling system. When I met the dealer who had sold her the car, I said that the heater core had been plugged by block sealer and that someone had put the block sealer in it to cover up a costly needed repair, and that it showed that the car had problems when she bought it, which led to the engine repair, and that he had made lots of money selling those warranties, and he ought to cover it out of his own pocket, at least offering to split the cost of the engine repair with her, as a good-will gesture. Again, in the warranty section, I discuss what we called the "crispy critter." Honda paid for that out of their "customer satisfaction" budget. This is what I suggested to the dealer. Well, he lit into me, said I didn't know what I was talking about, and that the heater core had been plugged by RTV (silicone sealer) used by her mechanic when he rebuilt the engine. POPPYCOCK! The dealer was showing his own lack of intelligence there. RTV forms large clumps that will not get into the heater core. They plug a core at the outer edge, and will be flushed out of the way by flushing and back-flushing the cooling system. The only thing I know of that actually gets inside the core, and plugs it up solidly, is block sealer. If the heater does not work, you don't want this car: end of discussion. (And yes, it is possible that a very low coolant level in the radiator will also cause the heater to not function, but if the dealer didn't even check that at some point before allowing you to drive the car, then you don't want that car OR that dealer. And in any event, a cooling system is, if it is working properly, a sealed system, and it will not lose coolant of its own accord, unless something is not working properly, and the most likely something is a bad head gasket or a cracked head, and cracked heads are very common among newer cars which use a cast iron block with an aluminum head, since their expansion rates are so different. It is also possible that the heater does not function because someone disconnected the heater core from the cooling system. The question then is why? The answer is most likely because it was leaking, and that again is a very expensive repair.) Again, if the heater is not working, you don't want this car: period, end of discussion.

Another way to buy a used car is to buy from a private party who is thinking of trading it. If you use the knowledge you have gained from this book to negotiate a better deal on the new car that he intends to buy, he might be grateful enough to give you his used car for ACV plus the tax on it. That would be a very good deal. Alternatively, you might be able to get the salesman to sell you the car for a nominal profit over the ACV, with a guarantee of sorts.... Legally, anything you buy from a dealer must be fit for its intended (or normal) use, unless you live in one of those dozen or so states that allow dealers to bypass the implied warranties of merchantability and fitness for the intended use, that are contained in the Uniform Commercial Code. When you buy something "AS IS" in Florida, for instance, you have none of the protections of the UCC, because business owners in that state control the legislature and the governor.

If you are buying a used car from any dealer, you know how to find the ACV for that car. You should be able to negotiate a fair profit for the dealer—though that would be more than the profit on a new car would be. Part of that is the fact that the dealer will have to warranty that car to you. Also, used cars are built one at a time, not mass-produced. If you want to buy the car, it is probably because it is clean, and looks well cared for. It would be difficult for you to find another example of the same make and model that you would like as well as this one. You can't just go and order one. Perhaps in the case of the ubiquitous Ford Escort, you could find another one as nice, and certainly if you can, you will have more leverage in dealing with the dealer. But in most cases, when you are looking at a used car, it is this CAR that you want, not just the same make and model. No doubt other people would have the same feelings when looking at this car, and that gives the dealer a lot more leverage. You must recognize that fact.

Financing the used car may be a bit stickier, however. Banks are more reluctant to loan money on a used car than on a new one. In many cases, the used car dealer will offer "buy here, pay here" financing. His interest rate will be very high. The dealer may also sell his notes (the loan) to a third party, who will be quick to repossess if you fall behind on the payments. This can be scary. Only sign that kind of note if you are desperate, or if the dealer will give you bank rates on the note. That way, he will be less likely to be able to sell the note at all. If you are buying a late-model used car from a new car dealer, he should be able to arrange bank financing for you, in which case the advice in the chapter on financing a new car is appropriate, with the notation that dealer's share of the finance rate is lower on a used car. And, of course, if you have a personal banker, you should talk to him or her about financing, and use them to determine the appropriate value of the vehicle. Credit Unions may be even better than banks in this regard.

Buying a used car without getting stung is more difficult than buying a new car, and I used to recommend that people buy new instead of used. The payments won't be that much higher, after all. The down payment won't likely be that much different, either.

The major difference will be in the length of the loan—and if you have a new car with a five-year loan, and a three-year-old used car with a three-year loan, the used car will be older when it is paid for than the new car would be. Of course, banks might be willing to take a chance on you for two or three years, but not for five, and they might go $4000, but not $14,000 or more, so there are other factors to consider as well. If you are buying a late-model used car from a new car dealer, you may be purchasing a transferable warranty also, and so you should read the chapters on service and warranty claims.

CHAPTER 8:

THE SERVICE

DEPARTMENT

We have already mentioned that the service writer who greets you when you bring your new car in for service is paid a commission. I was shocked when I found out what these guys earn! The service manager at a large, but not gargantuan, Ford dealership told me that his service writers earn from $2000 to $4000 per month in commissions. That was back in the late 1980s, so the number would be much higher now. They make at least $50,000 to $100,000 per year. If you come in for a simple oil change, they may try to sell you a front-end alignment—which, by the way, is not a warranty item. In fact, this particular Ford dealership had just installed a digital sideslip meter made by Hunter, to convince people that they do need a front-end alignment. Some of what they advise you to buy may be needed, or may be something which should be done soon, or may be something you don't need at all. It may be so-called "preventive maintenance" which might save you money in the long run, but they might try to sell it to you more often than it is needed.

When work is brought in under the warranty, the factory pays a much lower rate than the rate charged to the general public. The going rate at most shops these days may well be in excess of $75 per hour to the general public (I know of a motorcycle dealer who reportedly charges $120 per hour and a great many new vehicle dealers are over $100 per hour now), but perhaps less than half that for work performed under the warranty. If the service writer earns a commission at the same rate for warranty work, he earns less on the warranty work than on the customer-paid work. Ditto for the mechanic, who is paid by the hour on a flat rate scale, which means that the factory had one of their mechanics, with good tools, perform the work on a new car, and assigned a time period as appropriate for that job, and they pay the mechanic for that length of time for that job, regardless of how long it takes to accomplish the job. All work billed by the shop is at the flat rate, even customer-paid work, which means you will always pay the same price for a particular job, no matter how long it takes. If the mechanic can beat the flat rate book for that job, he makes more money. This can lead to fast and shoddy workmanship, especially on warranty jobs. It is therefore in the interest of the service writer and the mechanic, to sell you work which is not covered by the warranty, when you come in for warranty work.

As an example of flat rate, I wrote up a brake job one time, which called for 3.4 hours of work. It was turned out in less than two-and-a-half hours. The customer was charged for 3.4 hours of work at the then-going rate for shop labor. On the other hand, if the car is older, and something is seized, and the mechanic has to take longer, he loses money. Under those circumstances, of course, he is likely to do some damage just to get the job done more quickly. The customer thus might pay more for parts.

The mechanic might also do two or more jobs at the same time. If he is letting your car idle to check for a leak (something that might not be flat-rated), you might still be on the clock while he is working on someone else's car. If the garage has someone who does all the machine shop work, such as turning brake rotors and drums, your mechanic could be doing a tune-up while your brake parts are in the machine shop. Both vehicles would be on the clock, which is fine if they don't charge you a separate fee for machining the brake parts, but if they do charge a machine shop fee, and you paid for the mechanic's time while the brake parts were being machined, you are being ripped off.

When the mechanic works faster than the prescribed time, of course, things often don't get done right. I wrote up a pickup truck with only 3000 miles on it, with only two complaints. The owner LOVED the truck. One of the complaints was that it pulled to the right. When I drove the truck around the shop to deliver it to the customer, it still pulled to the right, and the steering wheel was 90 degrees away from straight. That customer loved his vehicle a little less after that work, I would wager.

I bought a new Dodge D-50 Sport pickup in 1979. I complained about the front-end alignment when I took it in for its first service, to the selling dealer, a large Dodge dealership that reportedly was at least partially owned by the Chrysler Corporation. They did not fix the front end, although they DID move the steering wheel. At 9000 miles, with the front tires worn enough to be illegal, I took it to an independent tire shop near home, and he had the tires rotated, and the front end aligned. The mechanic informed me that there were NO shims in the upper A-arms. He explained that the factory workers who align front ends are paid piecework, and so the faster they can turn them out, the more money they can make. They try to get them to the point where they go straight down the road, but they pay no attention to factors that affect tire wear. The dealer also pays his alignment guy a flat rate per alignment, and so he also checked only the most obvious thing, and ignored the rest. The independent shop fixed the front end properly. I was tempted to write Lee Iacocca himself a letter and tell him why I wasn't going to buy any more Chrysler products, but I never bothered. (After having owned a Pinto Cruising Wagon in 1977, I wasn't about to buy any more Ford products, either. My choices are getting limited. Luckily, my GMC S-15 was near perfect, and I bought that used.... And, for what it's worth, I currently believe that Chrysler makes the best vehicles designed and built in the USA, as a general rule.)

The mechanic is usually paid a percentage of the gross that he brings in. That percentage is usually half—50%. You think a mechanic can't make a good living, earning well over thirty dollars per flat rate hour? He can get paid for fifty hours of work with no sweat, possibly more, in a forty-hour workweek. That's potentially more than $75,000 per year. Of course, if say, 20% of his work is warranty work, which pays less than half of customer-paid work, that cuts substantially into that. And if he gets a lot of returns, he does that re-do work for free, and probably will spend more time on it on the second time around, in an effort to get the job done right!

I don't know the percentage of work that is not done properly the first time. I would imagine that 10% of the work is actually returned for correction. Perhaps the figure is not that high, but certainly some folks, disappointed with the dealer service, like I did with my D-50, simply go elsewhere, and pay for what should have been warranty work. For some mechanics, I would not be surprised if 50% of the work they turn out is substandard. The mechanic would probably be dismissed if anything close to 20% of the work came back for a redo. I remember when a popular Oldsmobile mechanic, at a dealership where I was employed as a salesman, was let go. I was told then that he had a 20% return, and that was simply unacceptable. The manager of a steak house once told me that fully 50% of his steaks were returned to be recooked, and they tried to undercook them, so that the meat did not have to be thrown away, since you cannot repair an overcooked steak!

I had two experiences with alternators that were interesting. On my Datsun PL620 pickup that I bought from an out-of-state dealer, I took it to that same dealer for routine service whenever possible. I noticed one time that the mechanic loosened the top bolt on the alternator, but did not raise the vehicle to loosen the bottom mounting bolt. A couple of months later, the alternator warning lamp on the dash lit up. I checked, and discovered that the bottom mount had broken. I tried to find a replacement at several local dealerships, and nobody had it in stock. Rather than ordering it, I called my selling dealer friend, and they had that part in stock, and in fact, they told me that they sell a lot of them! They shipped me one, and I had it at least as fast as I could have obtained it locally.

That engine came out of the 510 sedan, but the motor mounts were different on the pickup truck, so Datsun made a bottom alternator mount that was fabricated from steel, instead of cast in aluminum. The steel mount could not handle the stress of having the mechanic loosen the top mount only. Using a large pry bar and putting stress on the bottom mount while tightening the top mount caused the bottom mount to fail. My local dealers were adjusting the alternator properly, and were not having these failures, but my dealer friend out of state had a bunch of mechanics who were trying to save a few minutes adjusting the alternator, and they were selling a whole lot of replacement bottom mounts as a result. Another time I purchased a Mazda 323 off the auction line at a local Honda car dealership. The alternator was not functioning when I bought it, but for some reason the warning light did not come on. I had been badly injured in a motorcycle accident (a woman pulled a left turn right in front of me while apparently talking on her cell phone) and I was unable to replace the alternator myself. The dealer refused to help me because he had supposedly given me such a good deal on the car. (I later discovered that my friend the salesman, had lied to me about the ACV on the car, by about $250.) The dealer finally agreed to install the replacement part if I would pay for the alternator, either by buying it myself, or paying him his cost. I bought the part, getting a dealer discount from the counterman, who was buying motorcycle parts from me at the time, and thought I deserved a dealer discount, and he got fired for selling it to me at a discount. The car dealer installed the new alternator, and I picked the car up. A few weeks later, the alternator quit as I was making a left turn. I had healed enough to check it out, and it turned out that the dealer had let their used-car cleanup guy do the work, instead of one of their regular line mechanics, and he had forgotten to tighten the bottom mount after he adjusted the belt. When I made that turn, the bolt fell out (the nut having fallen off long before that time), and the belt started slipping. I found another bolt and fixed it. The message here is that if something goes wrong soon after you had your vehicle serviced, you should assume that the problem was related to the service job and complain to the dealership that did the service work. If they argue that it was not their fault, you should make them prove that. In these two instances, damage that occurred shortly after service at the dealership was related to shoddy workmanship at the dealership.

And therein lies the message. RETURN SHODDY WORK! Come back first thing the next morning, and complain, Complain, COMPLAIN! You won't need an appointment: they'll work you in somehow. The work will be turned over to the same mechanic who did it the first time, and he will be told to make it right, and he will not be paid for it the second time around. The squeakiest wheel gets the grease. You be sure to make a lot of noise. Demand to see the service manager, or the owner of the dealership. Make sure that someone in a position of responsibility and authority goes out in the car with you, and verifies your complaint. This might be the service writer the first time back, but if you have to come back more than once, make sure that the service manager himself understands what you are complaining about. Write or phone the owner of the dealership, and write or phone the factory complaint line. I know some people don't feel comfortable making that much noise, but you paid for a perfect car, and that is what you are entitled to have. Customers who do not complain are ignored. That is the nature of the business.

One time, I applied for a job as a service writer. When I showed up for work on the appointed day, I discovered that they had hired someone else after they had hired me. The other person had experience in that position, while I did not. (I had worked as service manager in two much smaller dealerships, I had also worked as a parts manager, and did most of my own repairs, had a college engineering background, and had sold cars as well as various items ranging from cameras, to appliances, to mobile homes.) They kept me around just long enough to determine that the other new hire was not a total toad, and then they let me go. Human beings are just fodder to a typical car dealership. Of the three service writers there (four, counting myself), none had been there a month yet. High turnover of personnel is fairly typical, and means that you should avoid the dealership if at all possible. I can't tell you any sure way to determine this, except to shop them for several months before buying, or ask friends who have bought there if that is a problem at the dealership in question. When I arrived to pick up my check, one of the mechanics told me he was sorry to hear about what happened to me. I replied that car dealerships operate in a fixed way, and when you have been around them long enough, you know what to expect. I knew what was happening, though I didn't want to admit it to myself, when I showed up on Monday to start work. When you hire someone who has no actual recent experience in the position, I think any reasonable person would agree that you owe the person more than four days to see if he can learn the position. The fact is, as I see it, that I became nothing more than a fallback position, in case the later new hire didn't work out for some reason. In virtually any other business, where they have three people doing a specific job, if they got into a position where all three had been on the job less than a month, the owner would want to know why. Often car dealers treat employees worse than they treat their customers—and it shows in the type of after-sale service that you receive.

So, the name of the game is that an attempt will be made to sell you work that you don't need when you come in. That is because of the pay plan that the service writer works under, enhanced by the plan under which the mechanics themselves work. Work will be done hurriedly because of the pay plan under which the mechanics are paid. What do you do? If the service writer tries to sell you non-warranty work that you feel is unnecessary, tell him that you want a second opinion. Before you authorize any work, take the vehicle to an independent shop. You should, of course, be careful to check out the independent shop also, either with the Better Business Bureau, or with friends, or with the state's consumer advocate, usually a department under the attorney general. If the dealership has been in business a long time, he probably has kept customers satisfied, but that's not a guarantee, either. If the independent says you ought to have the work done, he may be just drumming up business also. Ask both shops for a quote. If the price is close, have it done by the dealer, because you have more leverage there. You can always contact the manufacturer. If the independent is a reputable shop, and offers a significantly lower price, and the work won't affect anything under warranty, let the independent do the work. Make sure he uses American made parts where possible, unless the dealer would also use Chinese parts. And you might tell the dealer why he did not get the work. If work is not done properly, scream bloody murder at whoever is in charge.

These pointers might not save you a lot of money, though if you do have a lot of work done by independents, you might save considerable money over the life of the car. My advice would be to have the dealer do ONLY the warranty work, unless he is very close to the price of the independents. That alone could save you hundreds of dollars over the life of the car. It means extra work for you, but you wouldn't have brain surgery done without a second opinion, would you? As far as using genuine factory parts goes, if the dealer does not have the genuine part in stock, he will try to obtain a local replacement to get your car completed and out the door as soon as possible. So, taking it to a dealer is no guarantee of factory parts—and the independent can use factory parts if you ask him to.

CHAPTER 9:

WARRANTIES AND

WARRANTY WORK

When you buy a new car, it comes with a manufacturer's warranty, which may be as long as 100,000 miles on the power train, but the rest of the car may not be covered nearly that well—often for just 12 months or 12,000 miles.

Don't let a salesman tell you that if you buy elsewhere, you can't have warranty service done at this dealership. The service department is a profit center, and the service manager wants you as a customer, even if the sales manager did not. The service department will turn a profit on you even if you bought the car out of town. There may well be a provision that this dealership does not have to provide warranty service, and can make you take it to the selling dealer, but ONLY if the selling dealer is within 50 miles. Outside of that, don't worry about it, with most manufacturers. And you may very well be able to talk the service manager into honoring the warranty for you. In fact, if you have your warranty card properly filled out and available, the service writer who greets you when you come in for service might possibly have no idea where you bought the car, and in fact, is likely to assume that you bought it from this dealership. So, the chances that you would be forced to take it back to the selling dealer for service are actually quite low. Here, again, it is just the salesman looking for a reason for you to buy here, to keep you from shopping his price. Generally speaking, you can call his bluff with complete safety—and if they refuse to perform warranty service out of spite, you probably could raise a fuss with the manufacturer, and make them service your car, no matter where you bought it. But you might want to consider, do you really want these turkeys doing work on your car, if they didn't even want to sell it to you badly enough to earn your business? I bought a Datsun pickup from a dealer who was located 300 miles from home. I generally managed to get it to his dealership at all of the scheduled service intervals. Of course, at the time, I was doing a lot of traveling, in my capacity as a freelance motorsports journalist. I lived in Massachusetts at the time, and he was in Pennsylvania. Where are you going to go from Massachusetts, without coming somewhere near Pennsylvania? And his price, with my old car in trade, was hundreds of dollars better than I could obtain locally, and that was a lot more than I could ignore at the time. Of course, it helped that he had been a nationally ranked motorcycle racer until he was injured in an accident, and his son was, at the time of my purchase, a nationally ranked motorcycle racer, and I saw the two of them at all the major events I attended as a journalist.

The salesman will try to sell you an "extended service plan" which provides for all kinds of contingencies. There will be a deductible amount, meaning that up to that amount, the plan will not cover the work. The first $50, $100, or whatever the deductible is, you will pay in full out of your own pocket. This amount will cover most routine service calls, or the bulk of a one-day car rental fee. You will be entitled to generally up to five days of a rental car while your car is in for service and will be held overnight. This "warranty" is essentially an insurance policy, and carries a high profit to the selling dealer—perhaps 50% of the selling price, or even more, and certainly not less than 40%.

This is another profit center to the dealer. It is generally offered after the negotiation on the car price is concluded, so that you don't think of it as negotiable. If may even be offered by the finance manager, after you are done talking to the salesman. The price, however, is very negotiable. If you are interested in this sort of thing at all, chew the price down. Often the same type of coverage can be obtained from other sources, possibly your own insurance agent or your credit union. If you are at all interested in this sort of plan, check around and see what else is out there before you even go to the car dealership. Remember also, that this is a "single premium" policy, and that the premium will be financed in with the purchase, and you will be paying interest on it for however long your car note lasts—which probably will be longer than the coverage offered by the "warranty." Note, however, that policies from other vendors may only include the actual power train, and may be hard to find, or not offered at all, since the manufacturers increased the power train warranties on new cars, so compare plans and rates very carefully before you choose. And remember also that there may be all kinds of fine print, and these policies are notorious about not paying for repairs because they were caused by owner neglect or some such claim by the provider. Manufacturers have slush funds to cover such claims from owners who complain loudly enough, and some dealers may also have funds for that purpose.

Case in point: I sold a motor scooter, a new Honda Elite 150, to a young man whose grandmother used some Certificates of Deposit as collateral for the loan. He lost his job, couldn't afford the payments, and devised a scheme, we thought, to get out of making those payments. He assumed that his vehicle was insured against fire and theft. Now we had just performed the first service on the scooter, and one of the things the mechanic is obligated to do on a first service, is to tighten various nuts and bolts, including manifold nuts, to the specified torque settings. The owner gassed up his scooter one day, and said that shortly after that, he noticed that the scooter was on fire. He assumed the insurance would pay the loan off. But since the scooter was not the collateral on the loan, he did not require, and did not purchase, fire and theft coverage. So, they brought the scooter back, claiming that the fire was caused by a missing exhaust manifold bolt, which was NOT missing during the first service, and was properly tight at that time.

Further, the exhaust pipe on this vehicle extends up into the exhaust port. That is, the flange is not at the end of the pipe, so that with one bolt left on, there is no way that a live spark could work its way past the pipe, between the pipe and the port, then turn 90 degrees and make it around the flange and get out to some gasoline which he spilled when gassing up. That was physically impossible. Yet, in order to avoid a lawsuit, Honda eventually gave this guy a refund, even though Honda would likely have won the lawsuit, but there is no guarantee of that, and it would have cost them more in legal fees than paying for the scooter cost them.

I mentioned the lady who had to have her motor rebuilt after she bought a used car, and then discovered that her heater did not work, indicating that someone had put block sealer into the car, so it probably had a bad head gasket or worse before she bought it. She bought it used, from a very large used car dealership, which sold her a "warranty" with the car, and I believe that the warranty actually cost more than the car did! She brought it back, but the warranty company refused to pay for the repairs, because she drove it with no coolant in it. She had to pay for the repairs out of her own pocket, and the dealer refused to help her, and told me I didn't know what I was talking about, when I suggested they ante up for at least part of the repair cost, since it seemed likely that the car was damaged goods when she bought it. Since these repairs were needed very shortly after the purchase, she may have been able to cancel the warranty at that time and obtain a refund, but she did not want to spend the money for an attorney, and she would not have bothered to read the fine print on the warranty agreement. But those agreements usually do contain a clause that would allow the buyer to opt out, which might be governed by the laws of your state. Always read any document of this type thoroughly, and make sure that you understand the terms. Had she been aware of any opt-out period, it probably would have saved her a lot of money—about $1600 is what that repair cost her, and another $600 or more for the heater core, and as I recall, she paid $1000-$1200 for the car, and $1500 for the useless "warranty." Opting out of the warranty would have saved her much of what she laid out for repairs.

Another time, I sold a new Toyota Celica United States Grand Prix special edition. This car had been on our carpeted showroom floor for some time, and never leaked a drop of oil. One night, the customer called me after he said the brakes locked up, and the rear wheels locked up, and the car spun out while he was driving it. He said the tow truck operator told him it had to be something wrong with the brake master cylinder. I assured him that was not the case, since there is nothing in the master cylinder that would apply the brakes on its own. If the master cylinder failed, the brakes would not work at all. I asked if the engine still turned over, and he assured me that the engine ran fine. I told him it had to be that the transmission or the differential had locked up, and to have the car towed to us the next day. One of the complaints his parents had was that the car was leaking oil all over their driveway. We put the car on the lift, and discovered, and documented, a series of scratches on the bottom of the car, which started beneath the driver's seat, and continued back to just in front of the differential. The differential case itself was sprung, clearly because whatever made those scratches, most likely a concrete curb, had hit the differential case, which caused all of the differential oil to leak out. The parents threatened to sue Toyota to repair the car under the warranty. But this was clearly not a warranty issue. The kid "remembered" that he had hit something in the road, and thought it was a piece of two by four lumber, and ignored it. To make those scratches would have required something like concrete, and our expert opinion was that he was curb jumping with his new car. The matter was settled when his insurance company agreed it was accidental damage, and the insurance company paid for the repairs under the collision coverage. Always look at any possible angle to avoid having to pay for repairs that should be covered by another entity. But bear in mind that the dealer may or may not be the bad guy in this situation.

Other warranties, such as rustproofing, paint glaze, and fabric protection, are also underwritten by insurance companies, and are really single-premium insurance policies. These services are also negotiable—and bear in mind that the net cost to the dealer is generally 20% of the marked retail, so negotiation should include deep discounts. Certainly, you should not pay over $100 for any one of these items, and less than $300 for all of them together—well under $300 if the dealer does the work on his lot.

In some states, where such "warranties" are regulated by the state insurance commissioner, such as Florida, it may be illegal to sell such warranties at a discounted price. All you have to do in such an instance is to reopen the negotiation on the car price. After all, the dealer renegotiated the deal when he brought up these items in the first place. The policy gets shown at full value, even if that is the only profit the dealer makes on the car itself. Just make sure that the total you pay is LESS than the price that you agreed on for the car and the price of the "warranties" added together.

One thing that nobody talks about is phony warranty claims. I can't say how widespread this practice is, but I suspect that hundreds of dollars of the sticker price of every new car goes to underwrite phony warranty claims. Here are two examples: At one car dealership where I worked as the parts manager, a car came in for a transmission oil seal on a manual transmission. The transmission was removed for the repair, and the mechanic gave the customer a new clutch throwout bearing, without telling anyone except the dealership's owner and the parts manager (me). The customer picked up his car without knowing that he had a new throwout bearing for free. The next time a car of the same model that was still under the factory warranty, came in for an oil change, we kept the car all day. The mechanic had doctored the used throwout bearing so that it was noisy. He now had a "defective part" to return to the manufacturer. The owner of the car which had come in for an oil change was told that the mechanic had found that the car had a noisy throwout bearing, and that we had exchanged that part at no charge, under the new car warranty. No work had actually been done to the car, but the owner was pleased that we had found something he didn't realize was bad, and fixed it for him. We then filed a warranty claim for five or six hours of labor and a new throwout bearing. The mechanic got half of the warranty check when it came in, and the dealer kept the other half. We returned the "defective" throwout bearing with the paperwork for the phony claim, and then replaced it in our stock from the warranty check. If the manufacturer had contacted the second customer, the customer would have praised us for being so conscientious. But the costs of warranty repairs are a cost of doing business for the manufacturer, and so are marked up by the normal profit margin, then divided among all the cars produced by that manufacturer, and passed on to the public.

At another dealership where I worked, many warranty claims were turned in for labor only jobs, like gluing trim pieces back on, or resetting the idle controls because the mechanic thought the car idled roughly when it came in for an oil change, or fixing an exhaust rattle. These might be for as little as ¼ or ½ an hour. But even back in the sixties, this dealer wanted $200 per day in outright phony warranty claims. As Warranty Claims Manager, I had to get pretty creative to come up with that many outright phony claims. These days that would be like $600 to $1000 in outright phony warranty claims per day, and this was at a very small dealership. A larger dealership could hide more than that in phony claims today. Virtually every car that was under the warranty, which came in for service, had a phony claim of some kind written on it, while I was at that dealership. I heard through the grapevine that my replacement did two phony clutch jobs (at least $200 each for that particular car) in one day! And none of these cars had a lick of work done on them as part of that warranty claim; they were outright phony claims. The girl who put in two phony clutch jobs risked the manufacturer's rep coming in and demanding to see the parts the dealership replaced. Or the company could have asked the dealership to return the parts to prove that the work had been done. Apparently in that case, they got away with it.

And we, the customers, pay for every one of those phony warranty claims, believe me. What can we do about it? If the dealer tells us they found something wrong that we did not complain about, and that it was fixed under the warranty, it could be completely legitimate—but be suspicious. If you are certain that the problem did not exist, call the manufacturer on the toll free hot line. If the manufacturer sends you a follow-up form, to check on the quality of the service, and you were suspicious, say so. If the dealer didn't even tell you that the work had been done, that should be a red flag. The dealer should have given you a copy of the work order that was submitted to the manufacturer with the warranty claim. Be sure to inform the manufacturer every time that there is any chance that that the dealer made out a phony warranty claim on your car.

In another case, I had bought a slightly used (every car dealer has at least one customer who buys four or five new cars a year, and dealers love those customers!) 1977 (the current year at that time) Ford Pinto Cruising Wagon. I was looking for a vehicle I could sleep in on Saturday nights at the racetracks, when I was a motorsports journalist, and this was perfect. It was more like an old panel delivery van, with no side windows, and I fitted a curtain behind the front seats, and dark window tint to the rear window. I had a lot of complaints about the Pinto, and eventually, when I wanted to trade it, the trade-in value was extremely low because of the rumors of exploding gas tanks (which did not affect the wagons at all), so I had to hold onto it until some idiot totaled it on the interstate, one day, and he thought that I could not have survived, so he took off. He was caught about 25 miles down the road, and his insurance company got me out of it for full retail and then some…. At any rate, at some point, my dealer (now out of business) told me that there was a "silent warranty" program for owners with engine complaints. Apparently, some new college graduate employed as an engineer at Ford, told them that they could save about a nickel per engine by eliminating the holes in the top of the lower end bearing area of the connecting rods, which splash lubricant onto the bottom of the cylinder walls. So, they did that, and discovered that when the engines got some miles on them, they were getting noisy. I had never had precisely that complaint, and in fact, my complaints were more along the line of poor gas mileage and vibration, but my dealer told me that he was scheduling me for a complete engine rebuild, with new rods, new pistons, and new rings and gaskets, all under the warranty, even though the standard warranty had expired. This was a silent recall, and it was supposed to be offered only to customers who had complained about engine noises. But it was $400 in warranty repairs to the dealer, and this guy was looking for any way possible to generate additional income, so he set me up for it. In case any more such programs arise, you should be sure to let your service department know of any complaints you have, no matter how minor, but if they give you a warranty repair like this that you did not complain about, it might well be that he is just looking for additional income from unnecessary warranty work. You should advise the manufacturer of this.

I believe it is very possible that hundreds of dollars of the sticker price on every new car, support outright phony warranty claims. Some of these would be extremely difficult for the manufacturer to detect without the support of the public. If you have any questions at all about a warranty claim, notify the manufacturer.

You should carefully inspect, or test in any way possible, any repairs done under the warranty. Remember, the mechanic can make more than twice as much working on customer-paid repairs. Therefore, he makes an effort to turn the warranty work out even faster than customer-paid work. Warranty work may very well be shoddily performed. If you have any questions, contact the dealership owner, or the manufacturer. Make some noise. Often that is the only way to obtain any satisfaction. If the warranty is nearly expired, this is all the more critical, since the only warranty on the work itself is the dealer's own responsibility to do the work properly. Any comebacks should be brought in IMMEDIATELY. Do not wait to complain about shoddy repairs.

Saving money with warranty work? Warranty work is free, isn't it? How can you save on something that is free? Well as I have noted, warranty work is just a cost of doing business. That cost is paid by you, the purchaser, as part of the cost of every new car. If you find shoddy workmanship, or any hint of phony claims, raise a ruckus. This will help keep down the cost of warranty claims, which could help keep down the cost of new cars, And the cost of any alternative warranties the dealer might sell you is very negotiable, and that fact could save you hundreds of dollars off the price initially quoted by the dealer.

YOU ARE NOW READY!

It will be difficult to remember all you have read in this book while you are talking to the dealer. The biggest thing to remember is that he wants your money more than you want the car. Proceed slowly, and don't be forced into a hasty decision. You can always special-order a new car just like the one you want, if someone else buys the one that you wanted. (Of course, if you simply MUST have THAT car, and it is a leftover, or there is a strike, or the manufacturer simply can't build enough of that model, then you are at the dealer's mercy.)

But I do hope that this book will make buying your next car a positive experience, and that you don't lose your shirt in the process.

Other books by Crossroads Publishing of Florida

We have a website up and running at **www.cpubfl.com** . You may visit that website to find two reports on how to use the information in this book to save money on other purchases, such as furniture, electronics, photographic equipment, and appliances. The second report will tell you how to use the information in this book to start a business saving money for other car buyers. Check those out on our website.

We have several other books as well. Flip the page to see a few of them, and you can check our website for the most up-to-date list. For links to purchase these books, please go to the landing page for our website at **http://www.cpubfl.com**. We will be putting many more of these books on other websites, both retailers and aggregators. Links on the website will be updated as we do that. In particular, Jay's new book EXERTING INFLUENCE, which is a political primer for millennials not happy with the 2016 election, provides a roadmap for repairing the system for 2018 and 2020, and for influencing the reader's representatives and senators in the meantime. There is an appendix in the back which shows where to find your representatives and senators in every state, and where to find the full text of all of the laws in every state. This should be required reading for every new voter, especially, of course, those inclined to be progressive.

And PLEASE—if you have found the information in this book to be of any value at all—leave a favorable review on the website where you bought the book. Factual reviews are important to a struggling new writer or publishing company. It takes fifty reviews before book distributors will seriously help promote a new book, so this is of the utmost importance to us, to help us keep bringing you more high quality books like this one.

Jay Hamilton

COMING IN OCTOBER

COMPOSITION

Book One of John Waaser's Photography Course
Because a Technically Perfect Picture Without
Good Composition is of No Interest to Anyone!

Introduction:

John Waaser was the perfect person to write this book. As a student, both at Mount Hermon School for Boys and at Northeastern University, where he studied Mechanical Engineering, he was elected Vice-President of the camera club for two years running, four years total, where his principal duties consisted of coming up with the topic for each meeting, and securing the educational material for that topic from top companies such as Eastman Kodak and Ansco. It also fell to him to find someone to proctor the discussion, which about half of the time, he did himself. He later became a freelance photojournalist, and for two decades, he principally photographed motorcycle races, and other motorsports-related activities, including an occasional road test and other features. As a journalist, he showed an ability to take a highly technical subject and break it down so that ordinary people without a technical background could understand it. He took any number of portraits of up-and-coming racers as well. He did a few portfolios for models, and he photographed a few weddings. He spent about a year as assistant editor of a biweekly tabloid newspaper, where he wrote copy, took photos, set advertising, and laid out the pages. He owned Adpho Graphics, a photo studio and advertising agency, in the early 1970s. His personal hobby has long been night-time available light photography outdoors, where he frequently hand-held exposures of up to 30 seconds. He had his own photo lab at one point, where he processed film and prints including both black-and-white, and

95

color negatives, and color transparencies (slides) as well. He constructed a film dryer and an enlarger stand with variable height easel shelf, and published articles and photos of their construction in "Popular Photography" Magazine. For several years, he was listed on the masthead of "Cycle World" Magazine as their Eastern US Contributing Editor. He has owned a computer store, and has owned digital cameras since they had VGA resolution or less. He now owns an Olympus E-PL1 camera with two lenses, and carries several phones and/or tablets at all times. He also taught an adult education second-year photography course at a local community college for two semesters, while one of their regular professors was on a sabbatical.

Table of Contents

Chapter 1: General Discussion

I felt it important to discuss composition before even telling you how to operate your camera. For one thing, the owner's manual for the camera has more specific information in that regard, and you should consult that and practice using the camera until you are quite used to the functions of that particular camera. But the biggest reason why I thought composition was the most important first lesson, is that a technically perfect photo that lacks good composition is of no interest to anyone. I have sold photos for good money, that were lacking in technical perfection. I once sent a 120 roll-film transparency to "Cycle" Magazine, without magnifying it to see if it was perfectly sharp. They loved that photo, and ran it as a full-page inside color photo. When I saw it in the magazine, I was shocked. It was blurred very badly, possibly due to focus, maybe camera shake, or a combination of factors. I was absolutely ashamed to see that photo in print, yet they probably gave me about $300 for it (they paid ASMP—American Society of Magazine Photographers—rates, which were quite high, much higher than I was used to getting.) I questioned why that photo was run as a full-page photo, and they said that they loved the fact that three riders going around a tight 180-degree downhill curve at Bryar Motorsports Park in Loudon, New Hampshire, looking like they were stacked one on top of another, was unusual, and they just loved the photo, and thought it was deserving of full-page status in spite of its technical faults. There could be all kinds of reasons for technical problems, but when a shot is one-of-a-kind in terms of composition, and all of the elements come together perfectly, technical perfection is not an issue. People will love it. That is why composition is the first lesson in this photography course.

And composition covers any number of areas. The subject and how it is posed, is one big one, but the foreground and background, the lighting, and the color balance all enter into it. What leads the eye to the subject? What separates the subject from the background and the foreground? Is the lighting good? Is the subject at the best angle? Do shadows, or blocked up highlights, detract from the overall view of the subject? Is there a bunch of unimportant flotsam and jetsam around the subject to detract from it? The perfect photo must be carefully staged. A few small things might not detract too much, even though some will notice them. Case in point: the cover photo of this book. I should have stepped a little to the right, to center the sun into the dip in the tree line at that point. I did not notice that in the screen on the back of the camera while shooting, but I sure did notice it in the finished picture, when I blew it up. But that's wasn't a really major problem, and I was able to select the sun color to brush over the few twigs that were in front of the sun, and you would never know that they were there. I used a free app (well, I paid for the pro version, but you can certainly start with the free one) on my Android tablet to do that. The app I used was Photo Suite by Mobi Systems, who also make OfficeSuite and File Commander, both of which I have loaded in all of my Android devices. And I cropped the picture (using the tools in Microsoft Publisher, a free download when you run Office 365), and made some other changes that brought the sun to the center of the photo, even though the subject should ideally be one-third of the distance from the two closest edges for a balanced image. But I was more concerned with the cloud formation at the top, and I wanted it to frame the photograph, coming down the sides the same amount on either side. So I lived with the sun in the center. These are choices you sometimes have to make. I had dozens of photos of that sunset, and this was the most appealing one, to me. So I went with it, and lived with the minor faults that existed or that I created, in cropping it. It's also closer to the bottom than one-third up, but it's close enough, and I wanted enough dark cloud up at the top to permit me to use white lettering. I had plenty of dark area at the bottom. I still have had numerous comments about how much people liked the photo on the cover. I have noticed that when shooting sunsets, where you point the camera is important, in determining the exposure. Your camera will have a way to set the exposure from the meter, to give you the best image, and then move the camera to get more foreground or background into the image. Usually this involves simply holding the shutter release partway down, short of actually tripping the shutter.

Composition is composed of many areas of concern. There is the position of the subject, the position within the photo itself; whether the subject is leading you to something else within the photo, or to someplace outside of the photo; lighting; shadows; color values; and a number of other things, which we will go into shortly. The more technical ends of photography will be saved for future books in the series.

This book will be available from various retailers on October 1st, 2017, and available for Pre-order starting September 1st. For more information and links, visit our website at www.cpubfl.com

www.ingramcontent.com/pod-product-compliance
Lightning Source LLC
Chambersburg PA
CBHW061149180526
45170CB00002B/691